Acclaim for Scott Christianson's CONDEMNED

"Unusually intimate and powerful." —NEW YORK TIMES

"A slim volume of indelible impressions . . . Highly recommended."
—LIBRARY JOURNAL

"Startling." —LOS ANGELES TIMES BOOK REVIEW

"Masterfully opens pathways for thought." —THE NATION

"If the initial response to Christianson's book and exhibit are any indication, *Condemned* may further erode support for capital punishment." —VILLAGE VOICE

"The important achievement of *Condemned* is not in theorizing about the death penalty . . . it is in forcing the reader to look at it up close and thus get a firmer sense of what it really, truly is. If you favor the death penalty, you ought to know exactly what it is you favor. Based on the book, I will tell you this: It is a horror." —SCRIPPS HOWARD NEWS SERVICE

"A stunningly brutal look at the death penalty and the way it was carried out in 'the most famous prison in the world.'" —METROLAND

"A haunting gallery of death house ephemera." —THE INDEPENDENT

"This should be read by death penalty opponents and proponents alike. The humanity of those condemned can no longer be hidden nor should the inhumanity of some of their keepers." —JUSTICIA

"Christianson's display of the death penalty's human dimension produces an emotional, visceral effect on the viewer." —BARNESANDNOBLE.COM

CONDEMNED

Inside the Sing Sing Death House

SCOTT CHRISTIANSON

NEW YORK UNIVERSITY PRESS
New York and London

NEW YORK UNIVERSITY PRESS
New York and London

© 2000 by Scott Christianson
All rights reserved

Library of Congress Cataloging-in-Publication Data
Christianson, Scott.
Condemned: inside the Sing Sing death house / Scott
Christianson.
p.   cm.
ISBN 0-8147-1596-6 (cloth : alk. paper)
1. Death row inmates—United States.   2. Sing Sing Prison.
3. Ossining Correctional Facility.   I. Title.
HV8699.U5C4   1999
365'.6—DC21   00-6819
                              CIP

New York University Press books are printed on acid-free paper,
and their binding materials are chosen for strength and durability.

Manufactured in the United States of America

10 9 8 7 6 5 4 3 2

For Jonathan E. Gradess

Contents

Acknowledgments

This project would not have been completed without the generous assistance of several individuals, organizations, and agencies. Two colleagues were immensely helpful from the early stages: Tom Rocco provided professional assistance with photography, and Audrey Bennett Steinhauer handled artistic direction. Without their painstaking, dedicated, and talented work, this project might have floundered. Others who offered valuable input included Tamar Gordon, Kelly and Scott Whitney, Peter Christianson, Serena Furman, Caroline Tauxe, Craig Watters, Leonard T. Perlmutter, Jenness Cortez, William Kennedy, Nikki Smith, Myron and Jetta Gordon, Tony and Carol Archambault, Barbara Millstein, Peter Galassi, Michael Magraith, Avery Lozada, John J. Poklemba, Ronald Tabak, Michael Whiteman, Kate Burgess, David Hess, Chuck Culhane, Bell Gale Chevigny, H. Bruce Franklin, and Aaron Carlos. Additional help was received from Jonathan E. Gradess, Charlie O'Brien, Barbara Baggott, Mardi Crawford, Barbara Ryn, and Terry Bobear, and from capital defenders Jed Stone, Russell Neufeld, and Barry Fisher.

I especially appreciate the feedback I received from the following board members of the New York Death Penalty Documentation Project: James Acker, Anthony Amsterdam, Hugo Adam Bedau, Bill Bowers, Judge John Carro, Deborah Denno, Richard Dieter, Bishop Howard Hubbard, George Kendall, David Lewis, and Diann Rust-Tierney. Assistance was also provided over the years from Dr. James Folts, Dr. Ed Weldon, Larry Hackman, Christine Ward, David Ladanye, and John Schoolfield of the New York State Archives and Jim Corsaro of the New York State Library. Special thanks to editor Eric Zinner and his colleagues and staff, especially Daisy Hernandez, Despina Papazoglou Gimbel, Elyse Strongin, and Jeff Hoffman at New York University Press.

This work does not necessarily represent the views of the persons and organizations noted, and the author is solely responsible for its content.

CLASS OF SERVICE

This is a full-rate Telegram or Cablegram unless its deferred character is indicated by a suitable symbol above or preceding the address.

WESTERN UNION

(20)

W. P. MARSHALL, PRESIDENT

1201

SYMBOLS

DL=Day Letter

NL=Night Letter

LT=Int'l Letter Telegram

VLT=Int'l Victory Ltr.

1953 JUN 16 PM 2 28

The filing time shown in the date line on telegrams and day letters is STANDARD TIME at point of origin. Time of receipt is STANDARD TIME at point of destination

=SYB048

SY=CB139 RX PD=CHICAGO ILL 16 115PMC

WILFRED L DENNO=

:WARDEN SING SING PENITENTIARY OSSINING NY=

AS AN AMERICAN MAY I HAVE THE PRIVILEGE OF PULLING THE

SWITCH ON JULIUS AND ETHEL ROSENBERG, WILL PAY MY OWN

EXPENSES ANSWER COLLECT WIRE IMMEDIATELY PLEASE=

=MARY BELL HERCHENROEDER 1055 HOLLYWOOD=

THE COMPANY WILL APPRECIATE SUGGESTIONS FROM ITS PATRONS CONCERNING ITS SERVICE

CONDEMNED

Introduction

From 1891 to 1963, 606 men and eight women were legally executed in the electric chair at New York's infamous Sing Sing Prison—more than at any other American prison. The capital punishment systems and procedures that were developed at Sing Sing established the prototype for modern legal prison-based executions, and the resulting media coverage helped shape public perceptions of crime and punishment, good and evil, and gangsters versus guardians of public safety. For millions of persons around the world, the Sing Sing Death House *was* capital punishment.

Some of Sing Sing's higher-profile cases received sensational coverage by reporters from newspapers, pulp magazines, radio, and newsreels, spawning more than a dozen major Hollywood movies that imprinted chilling images of the chair, the last mile, and other macabre conventions onto the minds of generations of Americans. The place was so famous that a letter mailed from abroad and addressed simply to "Sing Sing, U.S.A." was likely to find its way into the warden's hands. Already a household word a half century before the electric chair came on the scene, Sing Sing became the most famous prison in the world.

And yet, despite all the attention it received over the decades, Sing Sing's death house was one of the most closed, secret, and mythologized places in America—a closely guarded and rigidly ruled inner sanctum that operated beyond the bounds of public scrutiny or humankind, and a killing machine that ran seemingly on its own power and volition and according to its own irrevocable rules. Every facet of life inside was controlled and prescribed by the prison authorities. Outsiders were strictly forbidden to enter without a court order; even an FBI agent or top law-enforcement officer required official approval to get inside, and those wishing to witness an execution were thoroughly screened and allowed to attend only if they carried an official invitation.

Information was tightly controlled. Reports about the prison behavior and character of condemned convicts were left to journalists and scriptwriters to construct as they saw fit, with all the limits and imperatives of a morality play. Long after the executions stopped, evidence of what had really happened inside the forbidding walls remained buried in bulging internal files or had vanished into eternity.

On April 8, 1977, however, as part of an excavation of prison history and after months of official wrangling, a staff archivist from the State Department of Education was authorized to take custody of some dusty old official records stored at the Ossining Correctional Facility (Sing Sing) in Westchester County, about seventy miles north of New York City. Some of the boxes contained records relating to the death house. This removal of the cardboard boxes in 1977 marked the first time that behind-the-scenes documentation of the executions at Sing Sing had ever been allowed outside the prison walls. By then, the death penalty itself seemed a relic of the past; the last execution at the facility had taken place in 1963, and restoration of capital punishment in New York seemed unlikely. At most, the records seemed a fitting subject for eventual study by historians, but they did not appear to have much current legal or political value.

For several years the prison records remained in official custody, closed to all but a few viewers. Finally, after years of cleaning, review, cataloging, and accessioning, a collection of some of the records was made available to authorized researchers at the New York State Archives in Albany. The materials from the death house included copies of two receiving blotters for the period 1891–1946, a log of legal actions involving condemned prisoners covering the period 1915–1967, assorted other prison logs, and a selection of 153 inmate case files spanning the period 1939–1963. The Department of Correctional Services still has not turned over to the archives the records for the bulk of the inmates who passed through the death house during its more than 79-year history, and fragments of some of the files occasionally turn up in the hands of private collectors or are discovered in library holdings.

Despite its limitations and gaps, the archival collection offers a revealing look into the internal administration of capital punishment as it actually existed, not just as it was constructed by image makers or recounted by self-serving survivors. The case records cover part of the Great Depression, World War II, some of the Cold War and the prosperous 1960s, and the early civil rights era. Some files hold personal effects such as rosary beads and religious medallions, Social Security cards, frayed snapshots, and intimate correspondence. Each contains a standard dossier that includes the convict's personal and criminal history, medical information, psychological assessments, relevant court activity, previous prison record, secret surveillance reports, appeals papers, clemency requests, visiting records, intercepted correspondence, executioner's card, death certificate, autopsy report, and other data, making up an official compendium or master file that was intended to be accessible to only a few trusted prison officials. At the time the dossiers were compiled, nobody dreamed they would someday be made public. Now that they have been placed in the archives, some state officials do all they can to restrict access to them.

Wedged within the files are individual black-and-white photographs (mug shots), taken by a prison identification specialist, of each newly arrived prisoner. Each profile view includes the inmate's prison identification number, indicating the order in which he or she was received at Sing Sing, and the admission date. The frontal view captures the subject's facial appearance and emotional expression. Most new inmates in the photographs still wear the formal, out-to-court clothes they had on earlier that day, when they learned the verdict, received a death sentence, and found themselves transported under guard into the death house. As might be expected, some of the faces photographed show the full effect of these recent experiences. Many also bear assorted visible scars and disfigurements, accumulated over their brief but hard lives. Nearly all carry somber, sullen, or resigned expressions before an indifferent lens. Some seem defiant, some bewildered, but most appear struck by an awful realization. Although presented as numbers, the condemned in these pictures come alive as human beings.

For this book, excerpts from these previously secret state files and other records have been provided to form a sequence of images depicting life and death in the Sing Sing Death House, mostly during the 1940s and 1950s. But in many respects the images are timeless. Together with documentation that presents some of the state's internal evidence about the nature and administration of the death penalty, these records provide a rare and authentic glimpse of both the humanity of the condemned and the banality of the rules and methods of the executioners. The selections also offer occasional insights about the involvement of outsiders: witnesses, victims, and next of kin. The disclosures from officialdom are at once secretive and public.

Legal execution by electrocution was introduced at the end of the nineteenth century, during the late Victorian era and at the height of the eugenics movement. New York had three prisons equipped with electric chairs capable of ridding society of significant numbers of those individuals deemed undesirable. One of the instrument's inventors called the device "the grandest success of the age." Although the new method of killing was never used as frequently as some policy makers would have liked, multiple executions often were conducted on the same night. Two, three, or four condemned convicts—oftentimes "rap partners," sentenced for the same murder—would go to their deaths in succession.

Sing Sing's first electrocution was a quadruple one, involving Harris A. Smiler (a white bigamist and wife killer) and three other murderers: a black man, a Japanese sailor, and another white man. All four men personified various social and physical defects of the day. On August 12, 1912, a record eight convicts (six in one hour) were executed; seven were Italian immigrants, five of whom had been implicated in the fatal stabbing of Mrs. Mary Hall at the Croton Aqueduct, although another Italian man already had been executed for actually wielding the blade. Usually, the multiples consisted of pairs.

The most famous executions involved Ethel and Julius Rosenberg, condemned by the United States government for atomic espionage at the height of the Cold War; Ruth Snyder, an adulterous blonde husband killer whose demise in 1928 was surreptitiously caught on film by a witness's hidden camera and later plastered over the front page of the New York *Daily News*; and Louis Lepke Buchalter, the reputed chief of Murder, Inc. (the forerunner of the American Mafia), whose underworld reign was finally ended in 1944 when he became the most powerful American gangster to be legally executed. Other condemned prisoners were equally notorious in their own time, but their fame has not lasted.

Yet, many of those condemned were persons whose only claim to fame was the murder for which they were convicted. Some electrocutions apparently were so run-of-the-mill that they failed to attract any members of the press other than a regular reporter based in Westchester, who fed a standard account of the death over the wire service. Notice of some executions didn't even make it into the major city dailies, especially if the condemned man was black.

Hundreds more prisoners at Sing Sing were sentenced to die but spared for one reason or another. (About a third of those condemned cheated the chair, and in later years the percentage of prisoners winning their appeals became so high that the legal machinery jammed and caused the executioner to cease production.) One of those saved— Isidore Zimmerman—spent 28 years in prison after his sentence was commuted. He ultimately was exonerated and released, but died before he could collect a penny from any judgment against the state. Salvatore Agron, alias "The Capeman," was reprieved by Governor Nelson Rockefeller and later became the subject of a Broadway show. But they were the lucky ones.

Sing Sing's final electrocution, and the last legal execution carried out in New York State during the twentieth century, involved Eddie Lee Mays, a 34-year-old black man who was convicted of shooting to death a white woman on Fifth Avenue and ultimately was added to the list of electrocutions on August 15, 1963. Six years later, the last death row inmate was transferred away. Capital punishment fell into deeper legal disfavor and seemingly was abandoned. The fabled death house was converted to a visiting center, and the electric chair was consigned to a Virginia museum.

Today, most New Yorkers are too young to remember much about their state's version of capital punishment. But since New York reinstated the death penalty in 1995 and judges sentenced the first defendant to death in 1998, a discarded relic has returned to use. Today's statute calls for executions to be performed by lethal injection—poison rather than electrocution—and Clinton Prison has replaced Sing Sing as the favored killing place. But Sing Sing's death house history remains alive in the faces in the mug shots and in other paper traces that officials unwittingly left behind.

The following sample offers a look inside.

RECEIVING BLOTTER
SING SING PRISON

(1)

Number

Sentenced *Oct. 25, 1889*

Received *Oct. 30, 1889*

Grade

Name *Charles Mc Elvaine*

Alias *Charles Francis Mc Elvaine*

Alias

Received from

County *Kings*   Court *of Sessions*   Judge *H. A. Moore*

Plea *Ver.*   Term *Execution*   Jail Time

Crime *Killed Christian W. Luca a grocer - Knife. att. Burg.*

Term out by Commutation, Expiration or Parole.

Where born *Philadelphia, Pa.*

Age *20*   Occupation *Driver & Printer*

Single   Married *✓*   Widower   Divorced

Height   Weight   Education *read & write*   Religion *Cath.*

Habits { Moderate / Temperate *✓* / Intemperate   Uses { Drugs *no* / Tobacco *no*   { Idle / or / Employed   { Father Living *Dead* / Mother Living *Dead* / No. of Children

Residence when arrested

Name of relative or friend

Office Card   Supt. Card   P. K's. Card   Number Book

PREVIOUS COMMITMENTS

Discharged for new trial May 7, 1890. and convicted the 2nd time Oct. 1, 1890. Retd to Sing Sing for Execution

Executed Feb. 8, 1892

Receiving blotter entry for first convict to arrive in Sing Sing Death House, 1889

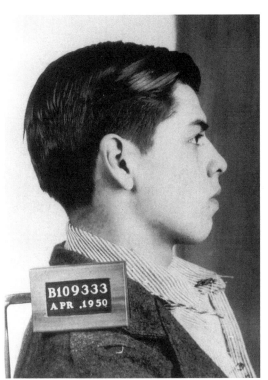

Ossining, N.Y. Sing Sing Prison & Hudson River.

Sing Sing

Built on the banks of the Hudson River in Westchester County in 1825, Sing Sing Prison already had become internationally famous by the time Alexis de Tocqueville visited it in 1831. Much of the institution's early success was due to brutal slavery, which helped make it profitable for a short time. By the late nineteenth century hundreds of convicts had perished, with causes of death ranging from consumption to starvation, suicide, and physical abuse, including water torture in the infamous shower bath, a non-electric and, usually, nonfatal precursor of the electric chair. Legal executions at Sing Sing did not begin until 1891, using the new method of electrocution that recently had been tested at Sing Sing and first was used at another New York prison, Auburn, in 1890. During the first four decades of executions at Sing Sing, the death house consisted of a section of the prison that was appropriated as the Condemned Cells. But a rash of daring escapes, including the violent breakout of condemned murderer Oreste Shillitoni, who killed a prison guard and seriously wounded another before he was quickly recaptured and executed in 1916, prompted the construction of a special state-of-the-art prison within a prison.

Prison officials at the gate

Interior cellblock

Convict in Sing Sing's 19th-century torture chair, the shower bath

Warden's office interior

Death house exterior

Death House

The new death house, designed by state architect Lewis F. Pilcher, was pressed into service in February 1922. Made of brick and stone, with steel bars encasing the windows of all 39 cells (including three for women), it was quickly proclaimed by *The New York Times* to be, "as far as possibility of escape is concerned, the most impregnable penal institution in the world." Under the new arrangement, a prisoner could not see another convict from his or her cell. The residents were divided into three classes: the newly arrived condemned; the pre-execution class, who had lost their legal appeals and faced almost certain death; and those who were physically or mentally ill. Six radiating cells, located near the execution chamber, served as a staging area (known as the Dancehall) for the electrocutions. The killing procedure called for the contract executioner to be hidden in a small room adjoining the electric chair within the chamber. The self-contained facility also included tiny exercise yards, a hospital room, a dental room, a keeper's room, a kitchen, chaplains' and doctors' offices, a reception room, and a meeting room for use by the governor, a judge, the lunacy commission, or other officials— everything needed for a modern killing center.

Here are done to death an average of ten men a year, although last year, 1932, twenty men were executed. At present there are 18 men and two women in the Death House awaiting the fateful day. These facts, in themselves, mean little. If they signified that only ten or twenty murders were committed each year in New York State, then one could say correctly perhaps, that the death penalty in capital cases was effective and accomplished its purpose. But actually far less than 1% of those who commit murder are executed.

—Warden Lewis E. Lawes, *Sing Sing* (1933)

Warden Lewis Lawes, who ran Sing Sing from 1920 to 1941, published several best-selling books against capital punishment and was simultaneously the nation's leading administrator and opponent of the death penalty.

Martha Jule Beck arriving at Sing Sing's front gate, 1949

Arrival

New York law required every capital defendant to receive a trial by jury, removed sentencing discretion in cases of first-degree murder, and guaranteed at least one automatic appeal from New York's highest court. For several decades, the legal process generally moved so briskly that a defendant was charged, tried, convicted, and executed within a few months of his capital crime. (Several would die before their eighteenth birthday.)

Most condemned criminals were slipped into the prison without fanfare. But sometimes crowds of curious onlookers and paparazzi gathered at the front gate to witness the arrival of a notorious criminal such as Martha Jule Beck or Julius Rosenberg. All new arrivals were brought directly to the death house, where most would remain until their execution. Once inside, the transporting police transferred custody of the "living body" (as the condemned was often called) to the state prison authorities, and the death warrant and other necessary papers were handed over and examined. Each condemned prisoner was meticulously photographed, physically examined, measured, and interrogated. All were asked to state the reason they had committed the crimes for which they stood convicted and sentenced to death, and these responses were also officially recorded. (As many as 40 percent claimed they were not guilty.) Eventually, each convict was escorted to a separate cell.

Some of those arriving appeared mentally deranged, and some came still protesting their innocence. Some were recovering from gunshot wounds or other injuries received during their capture. A few had been the subject of immense publicity or special prison alerts. Mentally retarded or cunning, young or old, black or Chinese, infamous or nondescript—they all came to meet the same end.

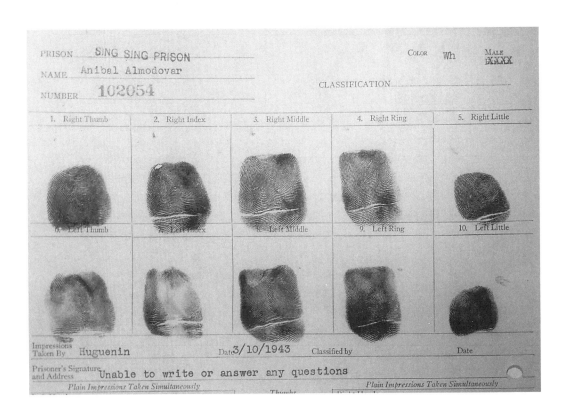

PRISON   SING SING PRISON   COLOR   Wh   MALE

NAME   Anibal Almodovar

NUMBER   102054   CLASSIFICATION

| 1. Right Thumb | 2. Right Index | 3. Right Middle | 4. Right Ring | 5. Right Little |
| 6. Left Thumb | 7. Left Index | 8. Left Middle | 9. Left Ring | 10. Left Little |

Impressions Taken By Huguenin   Date 3/10/1943   Classified by   Date

Prisoner's Signature and Address Unable to write or answer any questions

Plain Impressions Taken Simultaneously   Thumbs   Plain Impressions Taken Simultaneously

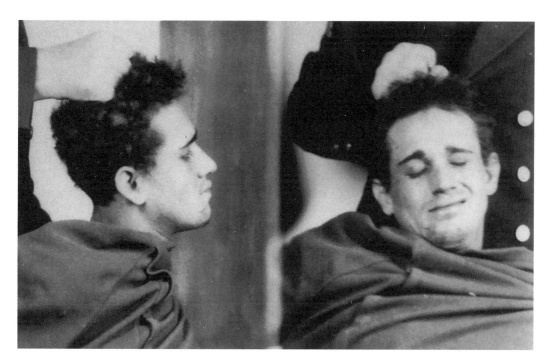

Anibal Almodovar arrived in a straitjacket, unable to cooperate for his admission procedures.

NAME:	Anibal Almodovar
NUMBER:	101–054
BORN:	11–3–21 (Ponce, PR)
AGE:	21
EDUCATION:	4th grade, Spanish
OCCUPATION:	Unemployed
CRIME:	Strangled his wife, Louisa, in park, night
CLAIMS:	Innocent, framed by detectives
JUDGE:	Donnellan, NY General Sessions
SENTENCED:	3–10–43
RECEIVED:	3–10–43
EXECUTED:	9–16–43

THE INNOCENT

Many condemned prisoners freely admitted their guilt, but an undetermined number of those saved or executed were doubtless innocent of the crimes for which they had been sentenced to death. Under today's stricter rules of evidence and other legal standards, a large percentage of the prisoners in the Sing Sing Death House probably would not have been sentenced to die. Court records reveal many who were questioned without a defense lawyer present, held for long periods under harrowing conditions, convicted on the basis of coerced confessions, identified in one-man lineups, or nailed by illegally obtained evidence that was not excluded as fruit from a poisonous tree. Many nonwhite defendants were convicted by all-white juries from which blacks and all other persons of color had been deliberately barred. Youthful first-time offenders were sent to their deaths without any mitigating evidence presented in their favor; severely retarded, mentally ill, or seemingly insane persons were held criminally responsible and killed. Some may have been framed; others were simply done in by lousy, lazy lawyers. Shortly before going to their deaths, a few convicts confessed their guilt but signed affidavits for the chaplain in which they swore that others also condemned were innocent. One individual whom some scholars have alleged was wrongfully convicted and executed was Charles Sberna, a parolee who was sent to his death with Salvatore Gati. Some archival records may support that assertion. Yet the state has never admitted killing an innocent person.

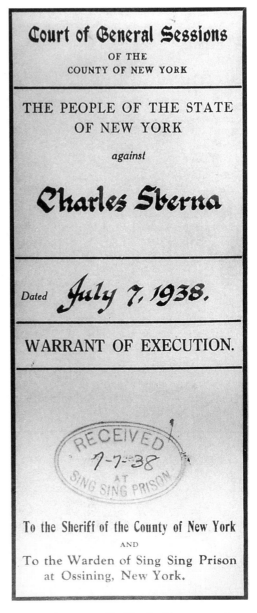

Death warrant for Charles Sberna, 1938

NAME:	Charles Sberna
NUMBER:	95–270
BORN:	3–5–09
AGE:	29
OCCUPATION:	Upholsterer
EDUCATION:	7th grade
CRIME:	Shot Patrolman Wilson, day, street, holdup
ACCOMPLICE:	Salvatore Gati 95–271
CLAIMS:	Denies guilt (NOTE: Chaplain McCaffrey reports that Sberna insists he is innocent)
JUDGE:	Wallace, NY General Sessions
SENTENCED:	7–7–38
RECEIVED:	7–7–38
EXECUTED:	1–5–39

ONE MAN'S CAPITAL CRIME: THE CASE OF DONALD HUGH SNYDER

In 1948 he was convicted of automobile theft in Hagerstown, Maryland, and served thirteen months in the Maryland State Reformatory. He was convicted of Grand Larceny, second degree, in Madison County, New York, for the theft of an automobile on October 28, 1949 and was sentenced to State's Prison for a period of two and a half to five years. He was serving this sentence at Green Haven Prison when he escaped on June 10, 1952.

Snyder, after his escape, travelled through the woods to the home of Marvin Arnold on Bullet Hole Road in the Town of Carmel. There he seized Betty June Arnold, a child of nine years of age, broke in the front door of the house and threatened Betty June Arnold and Mrs. Arnold with a view to forcing Mrs. Arnold to take him to New York City. While in the house Snyder obtained a china figurine and subsequently a carving knife, which he threatened the child with. By use of intimidation of Mrs. Arnold and fear for the safety of the child, whom he held in one hand with knife pointed near her body in the other hand, he was able to hold off the neighbors and police. The neighbors and father had pleaded with Snyder not to harm the child and he stated that he was going to take the child as a hostage and Mrs. Arnold and be driven to New York in the Arnold car. He threatened the life of the child on four or five occasions in the presence of many different people. One of the police officers had pleaded with him to give himself up and he refused, stating that the child was his "out." Holding the child at knife point he forced Mrs. Arnold and the child into the garage, which is attached to the Arnold home, and into the Arnold's convertible car. . . . Mrs. Arnold was seated in the front seat with her legs on the garage floor through the open door of the car. One of the police officers obtained a gun and after attempting to dissuade Snyder fired three shots, one of which struck Snyder in the neck and the other of which struck him in the chest. In view of the fact that Mrs. Arnold testified that the child screamed either just before or just at the time the first shot was fired, it is assumed that the stabbing took place at that time. The blow struck at the child was a forceful blow, penetrating to a depth of six to seven inches. Although the blade of the knife was 5-3/4 inches long, compression of the abdomen by the force of the blade caused the stomach and liver to be severed and the gastric arteries and duodenal vessels, from which the child died before an operation could be performed approximately two hours later.

September 22, 1952
Fred A. Dickinson
District Attorney, County of Putnam

NAME:	Donald Snyder
NUMBER:	112–748
BORN:	6–3–27 (Wampsville, NY)
OCCUPATION:	Transient
PHYSICAL:	5'7-½", 143 lbs.
CRIME:	Stabbed young Betty June Arnold in hostage situation after prison escape
CLAIMS:	Doesn't know
SENTENCED:	9–22–52
RECEIVED:	9–22–52
EXECUTED:	7–16–54

MARTHA BECK &
RAYMOND FERNANDEZ:
THE LONELY HEARTS KILLERS

Martha Beck and Raymond Fernandez furnished one of the most sensational sex-and-murder stories of the late 1940s and early 1950s. Beck was a skilled nurse who was highly intelligent but self-conscious about her weight; Fernandez had served with the Fascist forces in the Spanish Civil War before signing on as a spy for British intelligence in World War II. Both were con artists. They met each other through a pen-pal club for the lovelorn and entered into a stormy affair, during which they also teamed up to swindle and murder at least three lonely women. After their arrest, the "Lonely Hearts Killers" grabbed the attention of scandalmongers, including columnist Walter Winchell. The story ended with their demise.

NAME:	Raymond Fernandez aka Charles Raymond Martin
NUMBER:	108–595
BORN:	Hawaii
AGE:	34
OCCUPATION:	Construction laborer
MARITAL:	Married
PHYSICAL:	5'9-¼", 151 lbs.; tattoo ENCARNA across heart
RESIDENCE:	Grand Rapids, MI
HISTORY:	Served in military with Spanish Fascists; anti-sabotage service
CRIME:	Murdered Janet Fay by hammer and strangling, night, premises, Hempstead
ACCOMPLICE:	Martha Jule Beck 108–594
CLAIMS:	It was an accident and jealousy on part of two women
SENTENCED:	9–22–49
RECEIVED:	9–22–49
EXECUTED:	3–8–51

NAME:	Martha Jule Beck, aka Miss Lonely Hearts Killer
NUMBER:	108–594
BORN:	Milton, FL
AGE:	29
OCCUPATION:	Registered nurse
MARITAL:	Divorced
PHYSICAL:	5'8-¾", 202 lbs.
CRIME:	Murdered Janet Fay by hammer and strangling, night, premises, Hempstead
ACCOMPLICE:	Raymond Fernandez 108–595
CLAIMS:	Something I got into I had no control
JUDGE:	Ferdinand Pecora, Bronx County
SENTENCED:	9–22–49
RECEIVED:	9–22–49
EXECUTED:	3–8–51

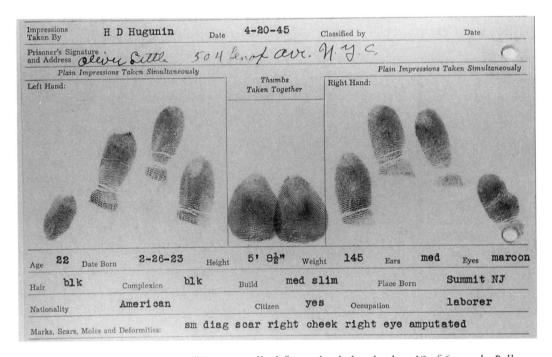

| Impressions Taken By | H D Hugunin | Date | 4-20-45 | Classified by | | Date | |

Prisoner's Signature and Address *Oliver Little*   *504 Lenox ave. N.Y.C.*

| Plain Impressions Taken Simultaneously | | Thumbs Taken Together | Plain Impressions Taken Simultaneously | |
| Left Hand: | | | Right Hand: | |

Age	22	Date Born	2-26-23	Height	5' 8½"	Weight	145	Ears	med	Eyes	maroon
Hair	blk	Complexion	blk	Build	med slim			Place Born		Summit NJ	
Nationality		American		Citizen	yes	Occupation			laborer		

Marks, Scars, Moles and Deformities: sm diag scar right cheek right eye amputated

"He is mentally defective, borderline level . . . IQ of 64 on the Bellevue Intelligence Scale . . . a high grade moron"

—Carl Sugar, psychiatrist-in-charge to Judge Goldstein, 4–9–45

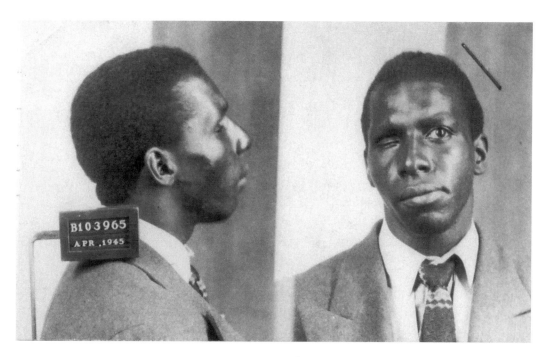

NAME:	Oliver Little
NUMBER:	103–965
AGE:	19
OCCUPATION:	Laborer
MARITAL:	Single
PHYSICAL:	5'8-½", 145 lbs; missing right eye
CRIME:	Stabbed Henry Beard, night
CLAIMS:	Self-defense, argument
JUDGE:	Jonah J. Goldstein, New York General Sessions
SENTENCED:	4–20–45
RECEIVED:	4–20–45
EXECUTED:	1–17–46

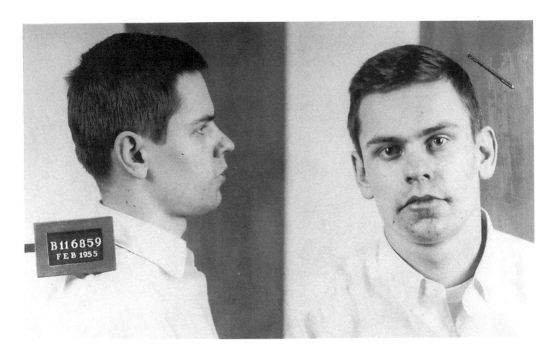

NAME:	William Byers, aka William David Snyder
NUMBER:	116–859
BORN:	11–10–36
AGE:	18
PHYSICAL:	5'10", 145 lbs.
EDUCATION:	2 yrs. high school
OCCUPATION:	United States Marine Corps.
NEXT OF KIN:	Mother
CRIME:	Stabbed and beat Anna Gresch, night, apt., 3–4–54
ACCOMPLICE:	Theresa Gresch
CLAIMS:	Only disposed of body to help girlfriend, Theresa Gresch
SENTENCED:	2–10–55
RECEIVED:	2–10–55
EXECUTED:	1–12–56

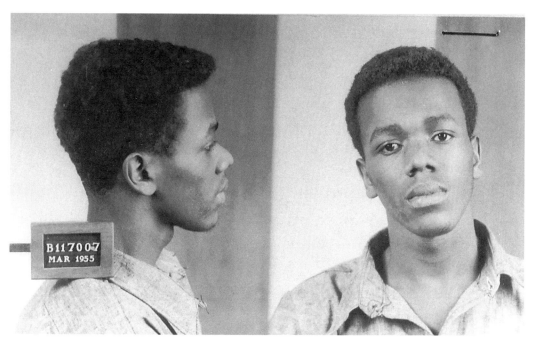

NAME: Norman Roye

NUMBER: 117–007

BORN: 9–6–37

AGE: 17

PHYSICAL: 5'7", 135 lbs.

EDUCATION: 5th grade

OCCUPATION: Messenger boy

CONTACT: Grandmother

CRIME: Strangled Isadora Goomes,
                     68, night, hallway, during
                     crime spree

CLAIMS: Claims innocence

EXECUTED: 1–9–56

NAME:	Edward Hicks
NUMBER:	100–630
AGE:	21
OCCUPATION:	Auto mechanic
CRIME:	Cut Max Graboff's throat during robbery
ACCOMPLICE:	Miles Hicks (younger brother), later reversed
CLAIMS:	Needed money
JUDGE:	Liebowitz, Kings County
SENTENCED:	1–27–42
RECEIVED:	1–28–42
EXECUTED:	9–10–42

NAME:	Alfred Haynes aka Alfred Davis
NUMBER:	101–864
BORN:	South Carolina
AGE:	26
OCCUPATION:	Stamper
CRIME:	Stabbed and killed his common-law wife
JUDGE:	S. S. Liebowitz, Kings County
SENTENCED:	1–4–43
RECEIVED:	1–4–43
EXECUTED:	7–15–43

NAME: Manuel Jacinto aka
                    Joseph Pinto
NUMBER: 100–701
BORN: Portugal
AGE: 48
OCCUPATION: Handyman
RELATIVE
OR FRIEND: None
CRIME: Shot and killed James
                    Monti and Mrs.
                    Delores Croyle from
                    ambush with double-
                    barreled shotgun
RAP SHEET: Disorderly conduct
SENTENCED: 2–13–42
RECEIVED: 2–16–42
EXECUTED: 9–17–42

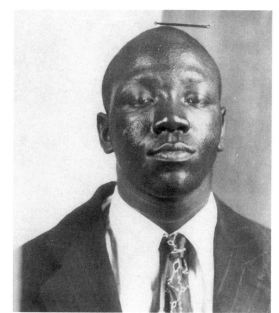

NAME: Arthur Johnson
NUMBER: 105–091
AGE: 21
OCCUPATION: Laborer
CRIME: Strangled, raped, killed
                    15-year-old girl, Rose
                    Palermo, night
ACCOMPLICE: William Washington,
                    also condemned
CLAIMS: Denies guilt
JUDGE: Liebowitz, Kings
                    County Court
SENTENCED: 6–27–46
RECEIVED: 6–27–46
EXECUTED: 4–17–47

GANGSTERS FROM THE "SYNDICATE"—MURDER, INC.

A trail of 21 gangster-related murders in Brooklyn's Brownsville section in 1939 eventually led prosecutors to a gang from the organized crime "syndicate" that the press dubbed Murder, Inc. After one of the alleged hit men provided grisly details about more than 200 mob-sanctioned murders, investigators nabbed a bunch of mostly Italian and Jewish mobsters. Two of the big fish, Emanuel (Mendy) Weiss and Louis Capone, ultimately were convicted and electrocuted with the boss himself, Louis (Lepke) Buchalter, on March 4, 1944.

NAME:	Emanuel Weiss, aka Mendy Weiss
NUMBER:	100—390
RELIGION:	Hebrew
PHYSICAL:	6' ¾", 221 lbs.
OCCUPATION:	Hat salesman
CRIME:	Shot Joseph Rosen, proprietor of candy store, a potential witness, 9—13—36
CLAIMS:	Denies commission
JUDGE:	Taylor, Kings County
SENTENCED:	12—2—41
RECEIVED:	12—3—41
EXECUTED:	3—4—44

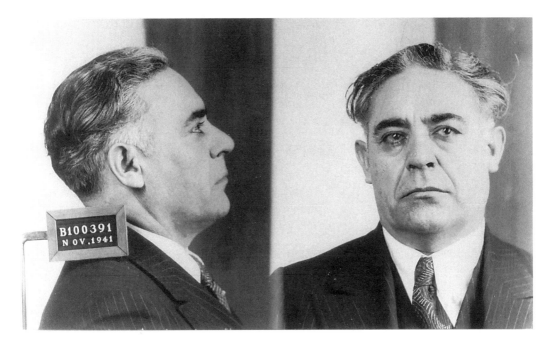

NAME:	Louis Capone
NUMBER:	100–391
BORN:	Naples, Italy
AGE:	45
OCCUPATION:	Proprietor, Orient Danceland
CRIME:	Shot Joseph Rosen, proprietor of candy store, potential witness, 9–13–36
CLAIMS:	Denies commission
JUDGE:	Taylor, Kings County
SENTENCED:	12–2–41
RECEIVED:	12–3–41
EXECUTED:	3–4–44

LEPKE: THE BIGGEST CATCH

Looking more like a prosperous clothier than the nation's most-wanted criminal, Louis Lepke Buchalter used columnist Walter Winchell as an intermediary to surrender himself to FBI director J. Edgar Hoover at the corner of Fifth Avenue and Twenty-Eighth Street in Manhattan. After a series of dramatic trials and appeals, he finally faced execution for having ordered the shooting of garment trucker Joseph Rosen. Sing Sing's Jewish chaplain requested that Governor Thomas Dewey delay Lepke's execution another day so it wouldn't fall on the Jewish Sabbath, but Dewey, the ex-racketbuster, refused. After his final appeal was turned down by the U.S. Supreme Court and his desperate efforts to reveal secrets about relationships between the syndicate and politicians also failed to turn the tide, Lepke calmly went to his death in front of 22 newspapermen.

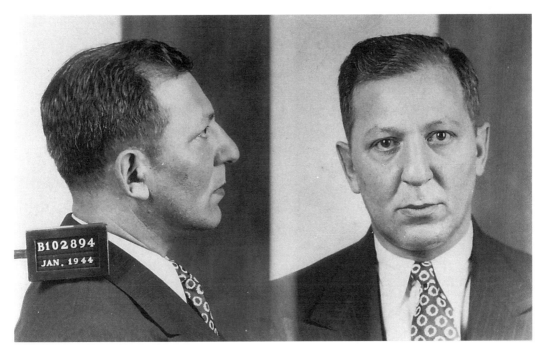

NAME:	Louis Lepke Buchalter aka Lepke
NUMBER:	102–894
AGE:	44
PHYSICAL:	5' 8", 181 lbs.
OCCUPATION:	Retired clothier
MARITAL:	Married, one child
RELIGION:	Jewish
CRIME:	Shot Joseph Rosen, revolver
ACCOMPLICES:	Weiss, Capone, Strauss, others
CLAIMS:	Newspaper notoriety
JUDGE:	Taylor, Kings County
SENTENCED:	12–2–41
RECEIVED:	1–21–44
EXECUTED:	3–4–44

When Replying Sign Your Full Name and Address. Give Inmate's Full Name and Number

Name *Chief Justice Lehman*

Street & No. *Court of Appeals*

City *Albany*   State *N. Y.*

354 Hunter St.
Ossining, N. Y.

Date *7/22/44*

Dear Sir:

I take liberty to write you and ask you to Believe me and to Help "Lew york Hing", Because He Had Nothing to Do with This murder. The one who Do the Killing in This Case is "me and Eddie." The Reason I lie to "judge Goldstin" and the jury During the Trail Because I'm afraid They Turn Something against me. And Because I figure I Can get away with out telling The Truth. But Now I understand it Can't Be Done. So I Now Tell "father martin" and you to Know There is Something Behind (may be Another Case like This) But what Ever is I Can't write it Down in this Letter. But I Do wish you to Believe and Call "father martin" in Sing Sing and He will Explane Eveything to you. And the Reason I ask you all this, is Because I Don't Care above my own Life. And in a way I Don't want To See innosent people to Dead or to jail for Nothing. please Help Him. Free Him. or Send Him to the U. S. Amry and Let Him fight He's Country. And Beside He's 100% good Citizen. and 100% innosend to Be free.

Thanking you in Advance
Respectfully yours
yun tieh Lee

102-807

From Yun Tieh Li to Chief Justice Lehman, Court of Appeals, July 22, 1944

NAME: Lew York Hing, aka Kelly Lew,
                Howard Chin
NUMBER: 102–808
RACE: "Yellow" [Asian]
BORN: Canton, China
CITIZEN: Alien
AGE: 18
PHYSICAL: 5'3-¾", 100 lbs.
RESIDENCE: Norfolk, VA
KIN/FRIEND: Frank Wong, Brooklyn
EDUCATION: 6th grade, China
OCCUPATION: Restaurant worker
RAP SHEET: No previous criminal history
CRIME: Struck, beat, choked, suffocated Mar-
                jorie Jasey in hotel, robbery, 1–24–43
ACCOMPLICE: Yun Tieh Li 102–807
CLAIMS: Bad company
JUDGE: Goldstein, New York General Sessions
CONVICTED: 12–7–43 [Pearl Harbor Day]
SENTENCED: 12–21–43
RECEIVED: 12–21–43
EXECUTED: 8–31–44

NAME: Yun Tieh Li aka Lee for Look
NUMBER: 102–807
RACE: "Yellow" [Asian]
BORN: Hong Kong
CITIZEN: Alien
AGE: 24
PHYSICAL: 5'7-¾", 130 lbs.
RESIDENCE: Chinese Seamen's Association,
                Canal St., NYC
KIN: None in U.S.
EDUCATION: 7th grade, China; speaks no English
OCCUPATION: Laundry worker
CRIME: Beat, choked, suffocated Marjorie
                Jasey, hotel room, robbery, 1–24–43.
ACCOMPLICE: Lew York Hing 102–808
CLAIMS: Bad company
CONVICTED: 12–7–43 [Pearl Harbor Day]
JUDGE: Goldstein, New York
                General Sessions
SENTENCED: 12–21–43
RECEIVED: 12–21–43
EXECUTED: 8–31–44

Monday, August 27, 1944

My Dear Warden,

I have never written a letter of such a serious nature before, nor to such an important person as yourself, therefore if I make an error of some kind, kindly excuse me.

Mr. Snyder, this letter is to ask a favor of you, and I'm writing directly to you, because I believe you are the only one who can grant a request of this nature. I am only a young girl of 18, and I'm not well acquainted with the technicalities of our laws, therefore if the request I ask is impossible, please pardon me for asking it. Just bear in mind that I had only good intentions in asking you, and my only thought was to bring a last note of good will to 2 condemned men. I know you are a busy man, Mr. Snyder, so I will get to the point.

You see, Sir, I read in Sunday's paper, about the two condemned men, Yun Tieh Li and Lew York Hing, who are about to be executed shortly, for the strangling of a woman. This article caught my attention, because I've known the two defendants for a long period of time. You probably think this unusual, that I, a white girl, would know these two young Chinese boys, for such a long time. Let me explain to you, that I was born, raised and am now living in a section of N.Y. known as Chinatown. That's how I've come to know the two men. They might not remember me or my name, as I have not seen them for quite some time.

I had heard of the trouble they were in some time ago, but could hardly believe it. They were always such fine upstanding boys, a trifle reckless, but not really dangerous. But Sunday, when I realized they were to be executed for *murder*, it seemed frankly, impossible. I know not the circumstances of the crime, but whatever they may be, I'm sure they must have fallen into some terrible temptation, and committed the crime by some accident.

Warden, they are not *killers*!! No matter what the verdict was, or how they were judged. I believe in my heart, that they could not *willfully* commit a murder any more than *you* could. Now I have to stand helplessly by, and watch two young lives being snuffed out, because of a cruel trick of fate! I grew up in the same neighborhood as these boys and came to know them as well as my friends and relatives. I could never have foreseen what life had in store for them, because if I had, I would have offered any assistance in my power.

Now that they are about to die, the only way I can assist them, is by praying to God to have mercy on their souls, and to be with them in their last hour.

I have written the both of them notes, which I have enclosed in this letter. The request I ask of you, is that my notes be delivered to them, before they are executed. I have left them unsealed for your careful examination. You can read them and see that they are perfectly harmless notes, and they may bring comfort in their last hour, to these poor condemned men. I beseech you, sir, to kindly have these notes delivered, for although this effort is of no help to me, I'm sure it will be beneficial to those boys, who are to meet such a terrible fate. I ask your kindest indulgence, in granting me this request. If it cannot be done, then I thank you just the same. I would be grateful if you answered this letter, and let me know whether my plea was successful or not. Thank you a million times.

Respectfully yours,
Helen Perrone

Request Denied
8-30-44

Rules

Rules governed every facet of death house operations. No one other than approved staff was allowed admittance, except by court order. Only approved persons were permitted to correspond with or visit a condemned convict. Incoming and outgoing mail was scrupulously monitored and censored. Conversations between visitors were often overheard and recorded by watchful guards. News reporters were denied entry unless they had been invited to officially witness an execution. By all accounts, the rules were strictly enforced.

Visitation Rules

IMMEDIATE FAMILY	(Father, Mother, Sisters, Wife, Children.)

Week-Day visits

Two days each week—any day except Thursday. (When original sentence of the Court is to be carried out, visits will be permitted on the last Thursday as outlined below.)

Sunday visits

Two Sunday visits each month, dependent upon the number of men in the Death House. One Sunday visit a month if the number of men increases.

(1) Sunday visits are to be limited to three visits in the morning and three visits in the afternoon. Two hours for each one.
(2) Passes for Sunday and holiday visits to be handed to the Principal Keeper before Tuesday.
(3) To be fingerprinted.
(4) Wife to present marriage certificate or a certified copy thereof.

OUTSIDE FAMILY

(Aunts, Uncles, Cousins, In-Laws, Friends.)
Number of these people approved for visiting to be limited to five. One visit a week from friends.

(1) To be fingerprinted.
(2) Must have a Court order.

Last visits on Thursday afternoon and evening are to be limited to members of immediate family. On either Monday, Tuesday, Wednesday (during regular visiting hours) or Thursday until noon time, one extra visit from friends. In addition, provided no immediate relatives apply to visit on Thursday afternoon or evening, visit will be allowed from friends who are on approved visiting list. *(This applies to last week only.)*

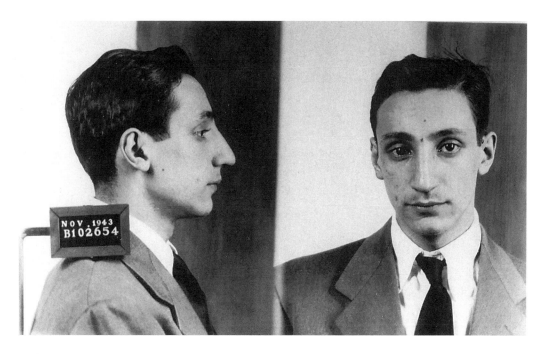

Frank DiMaria
#102–654
Condemned Cells

3–3–44

Dear Sir:

In reply to your note of recent date I am sorry
to have to inform you that rules and regulations
do not permit men in the Condemned Cells to
possess a Fountain Pen.

Very truly yours,
/S/
WARDEN

NAME:	Frank DiMaria
NUMBER:	102–654
AGE:	23
OCCUPATION:	Buttonhole maker
MARITAL:	Married, 1 child
PHYSICAL:	5'7-½", 124 lbs.
CRIME:	Shot Francis Servido in poolroom, day
RAP SHEET:	No prior arrests
ACCOMPLICES:	Alex Bellomo 102–655, Peter Delutro 102–656
CLAIMS:	Claims innocence
JUDGE:	Donnellan, New York General Sessions
SENTENCED:	11–2–43
RECEIVED:	11–2–43
EXECUTED:	6–22–44

This letter is returned to you because:

1. You did not sign it properly.
2. You did not fill out stub properly.
3. Name of addressee has not been approved.
4. Letters addressed to General Delivery not permitted to be mailed.
5. It contains Criminal or Prison news.
6. Begging for Packages or Money not allowed.
7. You are not permitted to receive the articles requested in your letter.
8. The articles requested can only be received new from dealer.
9. Correspondence with newspapers or newspaper employees not permitted.
10. You cannot have a visit with the person named in your letter unless approved by the Warden.
11. Inmate who wrote letter for you did not sign his name.
12. Special letters must not be submitted Saturday, Sunday or Holidays.
13. You did not stick to your subject.
14. You have no stamps on deposit.

CORRESPONDENCE DEPT., Per . . . . . .

This is to certify that the attached marriage certificate submitted in the above case has been examined under the office detectoscope and appears to be without alteration.

Memo from the Correspondence Unit, 7–12–38

December 5, 1952

Mr. J. V. Bennett
Director, Bureau of Prisons
U.S. Department of Justice
Washington 25, DC

Dear Sir:

This is in reply to your letter of November 24, 1952 with relation to the pending execution of the Rosenbergs. Procedure at this institution for State executions, is as follows:

After the order from the Court of Appeals has been received fixing the week of execution for carrying into effect the original sentence of death, notices are sent as follows:

1. Condemned prisoner.
2. Governor.
3. Clerk of the Court of Appeals (acknowledgement).
4. Commissioner of Correction.
5. Chairman of Governor's Commission, to examine into the mental condition of the condemned prisoner.
6. Various officials within the institution such as principal keeper, prison physician, Chaplain, steward.

In the interim the Governor's Commission calls at the institution to conduct their examination of the condemned prisoner. It has been the custom to schedule executions at this institution on Thursday the week of execution at 11:00 P.M. Notifications for the scheduled execution are sent to the Governor, Commissioner of Correction, Chief Engineer at this institution, and executioner. Also, in accordance with Section 507 of the Code of Criminal Procedure of the State of New York, invitations are sent to the following approximately five days before the scheduled execution:

1. A Justice of the Supreme Court.
2. District Attorney of the County of Conviction.
3. Sheriff of the County of Conviction.
4. At least twelve reputable citizens of full age, selected by the Warden, and may include newspaper representatives.

Arrangements are also made for the Warden, two physicians, Chaplain, principal keeper, assistant principal keeper, Captain, two lieutenants and three sergeants to be present. All invited witnesses, including newspaper men who have been approved by the Warden, are assembled in the Warden's Office at 10:30 P.M., invitations are collected, and satisfactory proof of identity established. After this has been completed the Warden issues instructions to the invited witnesses to the effect that they have been invited in accordance with Section 507 of the Code of Criminal Procedure of the State of New York, to attend the scheduled execution and that upon entering the death chamber they will refrain from talking, smoking, and making any unnecessary noises. Any person having in his possession any firearms is directed to leave them with the officer at the front door. They are also instructed, in accordance with Section 508 of the Code of Criminal Procedure of the State of New York, that upon their return from the death chamber to the Administration Building, they will be required to sign a certificate attesting to the fact that they served as an official witness at the said execution. A frisk of all witnesses is conducted in the Administration Building prior to their entering the bus to be escorted to the death house. In accordance with Section 508 of the Code of Criminal Procedure of the State of New York, the Warden's Certificate is prepared and signed by him immediately following the execution, showing the time and place of execution, in conformity to the sentence of the court and the provisions of this Code. Also at this time signatures are procured from the persons present and witnessing the execution. These certificates, together with the certificate of post mortem examination is then filed within ten days after the date of execution in the office of the Clerk of the Court (as amended by Chapter 671 of the Laws of 1949, effective immediately upon its enactment on April 18, 1949, certificates to be filed with Clerk of the Court, rather than the Clerk of the County). For your information, I am attaching copies of Sections 507, 508 and 509 of the Code of Criminal Procedure of the State of New York. Also, copies of Warden's certificate and witness list which are used at this institution.

Very truly yours,
/s/
L. J. Kelly
Acting Warden

encl.
LJK:G:g

From the Introductory Course for Custodial Officers *(Albany: Department of Corrections, October 1943):*

This is the general environment which surrounds the daily activities of the prison guard. He is thrust into a group of men being held under the stern injunction of law which they have violated and which he has sworn to uphold. His uniform is the visible embodiment of the power and authority of the state. Any challenge to this authority must be instantly and decisively dealt with by the guard, whose responsibility in each case is single and absolute. Fortunately, such occurrences in New York State prisons are rare because of the progressive penal policies of the state.

Guards

Three shifts of prison guards and other employees manned the Sing Sing Death House every day of the year, some of them for decades. Called correction officers by the state, they were collectively referred to as "screws" or "hacks" by the convicts. Most guards, of Irish or German descent, hailed from a handful of upstate prison towns. Some were second- or third-generation prison guards. All guards were white males. Prisoners and keepers subjected each other to relentless scrutiny, sometimes berating or coming to blows with their tormentors but for the most part keeping a wary distance.

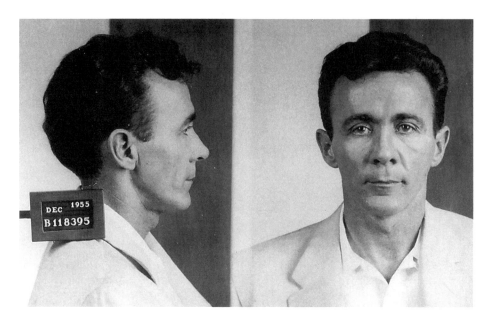

NAME:	Elmer Burke aka Trigger
NUMBER:	118–395
AGE:	38
OCCUPATION:	Laborer
PHYSICAL:	5'7–½", 142 lbs.
CRIME:	Shot Edward Walsh, tavern, night
RAP SHEET:	Very extensive
SENTENCED:	12–16–55
RECEIVED:	12–16–55
EXECUTED:	1–9–58

Oct. 1, 1957

I hereby report Elmer Burke, No. 118–395, Cell #7 E. Wing, Shop CC's for Assaulting an Officer. At about 10:00 AM while he was in the exercise yard Burke came to the gate and asked me to get him some bread, so he could feed some birds who occasionally fly into the yard. I checked with the CC Kitchen and found that were two slices of stale bread which could not be used for anything else and which would have been thrown away and gave them to inmate Burke. Apparently Burke was dissatisfied with this and when he came out of his cell for the afternoon exercise period he stopped in front of me in the Center Corridor and asked why I was picking on him in only giving him two slices of bread. As I spoke to explain he threw a punch at me. It was necessary for Officers Smith and Bosch to assist me in restraining him and locking him in his cell.

F. LORZ
Correction Officer

NAME:	Edward Kelly
NUMBER:	111–412
BORN:	8–31–99 (Rensselaer)
AGE:	52
OCCUPATION:	Machinist
MARITAL:	Divorced
CRIME:	Shot stranger Elouise McHugh with rifle on Main Street, Kingston, broad daylight
CLAIMS:	Lost control
JUDGE:	John Cashin, Ulster County
SENTENCED:	9–29–50
RECEIVED:	10–2–50
EXECUTED:	10–30–52

After his initial death sentence was overturned on appeal and a new trial was ordered, Kelly wrote this letter to the warden on June 12, 1951, as he was being discharged.

Dear Sir:

Due to the fact that I'm leaving the "Death House," I cannot say I have any regrets, nor will I recommend it to any one, but I can inform them that, if they are ever unfortunate enough to go to Sing Sing, they will be very well treated. I had no fault to find with anything or anybody during my stay, every reasonable request was granted. The entire staff of the prison are a credit to New York State. The Officers and Guards are as fine a group of men as you could find anywhere. "Dick" and "Freddie" go about their duties as if they had a part interest in the place, always helpful and ready with a word of cheer if needed. I enjoyed "Terry's" homelike meals. It would certainly be a pleasure to meet everybody, including yourself, under different circumstances. I extend my best wishes to all. But I hope I never come back.

Sincerely,
Edward H. Kelly
109–821

Kelly was reconvicted, sentenced again to death, and returned to the death house on November 28, 1951. He was given a new number, 111–412, and ultimately was executed on October 30, 1952.

April 15, 1958

Officer-in-Charge
Front Door
Admin. Bldng.

Dear Sir:

This is to advise that the Governor's Lunacy Commission, comprising Dr. John F. McNeil, and others, will convene at this institution on Thursday, April 17, 1958, at 10:30 A.M. Upon the arrival of the Commission, you are to immediately inform the Principal Keeper to this effect.

Very truly yours,
/S/
Warden

Shrinks

State law required a medical panel, the Lunacy Commission, to examine each convict personally, shortly before the scheduled execution, in order to perform the dubious task of trying to determine whether or not the condemned person had been sane at the time of commission of the crime for which he or she was to be executed. (Some crimes had occurred several years prior to this examination.) Convicts were also examined by other "shrinks"—the prison psychiatrists. Such relationships were not regarded as therapeutic or rational by the condemned, and it was only in the rarest of cases that the physicians involved officially attested to any problematic insanity on the part of those they examined. Instead, the opposing parties went through the motions of perfunctory clinical interviews. Then the doctors submitted their form reports.

NAME:	Frederick Wood aka Killer
NUMBER:	128–751
BORN:	10–29–11 (Vermont)
OCCUPATION:	Salesman
CRIME:	Killed John Rescigno with bottle, killed Frederick Sees with shovel
CLAIMS:	Says he hates homosexuals
RAP SHEET:	Extensive criminal history, served previous sentence for murder; history of suicide attempts
SENTENCED:	12–7–61
EXECUTED:	3–21–63

From a transcript of Wood's interview with the Lunacy Commission, December 18, 1962.

Question: Is there any way we can help you?
Answer: Let me burn.

After spurning lawyers' efforts to save his life, Wood went to his death on March 21, 1963.

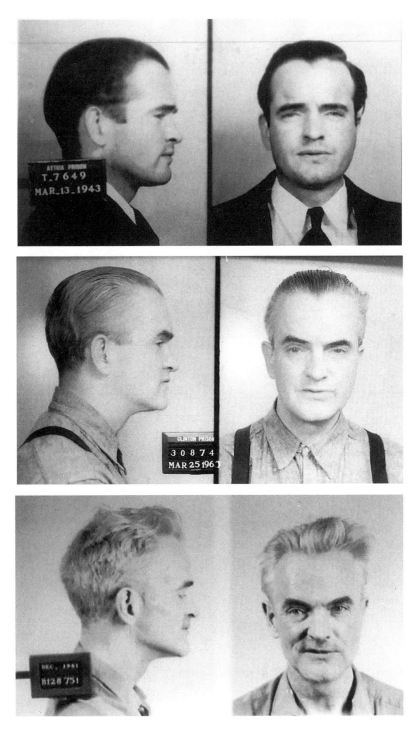

The prison aging of Frederick Wood: March 13, 1943 (top); March 25, 1960 (middle); and December 8, 1961 (bottom)

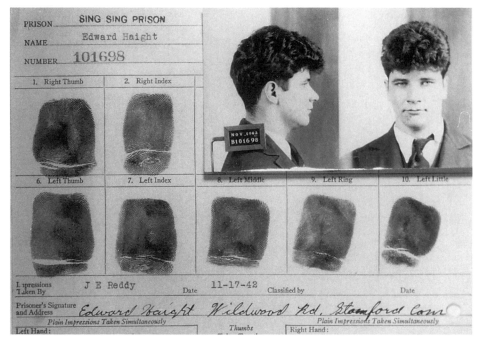

PRISON	SING SING PRISON
NAME	Edward Haight
NUMBER	101698

| 1. Right Thumb | 2. Right Index |
| 6. Left Thumb | 7. Left Index | 8. Left Middle | 9. Left Ring | 10. Left Little |

Impressions Taken By   J E Reddy   Date   11-17-42   Classified by   Date

Prisoner's Signature and Address   *Edward Haight Wildwood Rd. Stamford Conn*

Plain Impressions Taken Simultaneously   Thumbs   Plain Impressions Taken Simultaneously

Left Hand: Right Hand:

NOV.1942 B101698

Sing Sing Psychologist's Examination Report of Haight

NAME:	Edward Haight
NUMBER:	101–698
BORN:	9–19–25
AGE:	17
PHYSICAL:	5'7", 152 lbs.
CRIME:	Assaulted, murdered two girls, aged 6 and 8
CLAIMS:	"I don't know why I did it"
SENTENCED:	11–17–42
RECEIVED:	11–17–42
EXECUTED:	7–8–43

Examiner ....Argento
Age 17
Mental age...16.0
School grades completed ....1 year HS
Test results: Language: Alpha 16.0
Classification: Normal Type ....Unstable

Comments or test findings: Cynical attitude. Silly cooperation and quite efficient effort.

Impression: Normal level of intelligence. Anomalous character; intensive volitional and emotional reactions. Poverty of sentiment, purpose and ambition. Peculiar sexual reaction degenerating into chaotic sex. A readiness of psychoneurotic episodes from trivial causes.

Outlook: Doubtful; but environmental control with maturity, marriage and development of balancing forces might help.

From the Report of the Governor's Lunacy Commission to Governor Nelson A. Rockefeller, December 11, 1959:

As a result of their observation and final examination on this date, a consideration of the Record on Appeal, and as a result of the testimony taken, it is the unanimous opinion of your Commission that the said prisoner is sane at the present time, and they have no reason to believe that he was not sane at the time of the commission of the crime for which he was convicted.

/s/ John F. McNeil, M.D., Chairman
/s/ Leo F. O'Donnell, M.D.
/s/ George F. Etling, M.D.

Personal effects left behind by a deceased prisoner

Ties

Prison note cards dutifully recorded the names, addresses, and relationships of next of kin, relatives seeking to visit or correspond, and notations about children. Some inmates received no visits from family, and their own wives or mothers declined to claim their bodies for burial after the execution. Others were visited and written to as often as was allowed. Family relations were both complex and emotionally charged; so were attorney-client relations. And some prisoners attracted unusual interest, both sympathetic and condemnatory, from members of the general public, who wrote letters that ended up in the warden's pile.

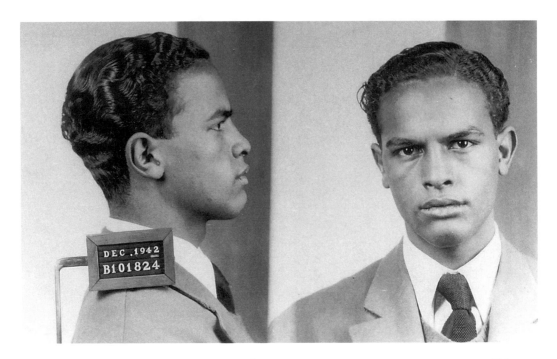

For participating in the robbery and murder of an American serviceman in wartime, 18-year-old Benitez DeJesus was condemned for "aiding and abetting the enemy."

NAME:	Benitez DeJesus
NUMBER:	B101824
BORN:	6–30–24 (San Tuce, PR)
AGE:	18
OCCUPATION:	Handyman
PHYSICAL:	5'7", 127 lbs.
CRIME:	Murder, stabbed Edwin Berkowitz, $6 robbery, 10–2–42
ACCOMPLICES:	William Diaz 101–827, Americo Romano 101–831
JUDGE:	Wallace, New York General Sessions
SENTENCED:	12–21–42
RECEIVED:	12–21–42
EXECUTED:	7–8–43

I heard that you have a new guard up there who is telling you that you have no chance—that you will certainly get the chair. I do not see how anybody can be that brutal. Even if he believed you would get the chair, he should not have told you, he should have used a little tact.

—"Kite" (written message) to De Jesus from a fellow prisoner

NAME:	Edward Jones, aka Sunny, Sunny Grayson
NUMBER:	104–778
PHYSICAL:	5'7-½", 173 lbs.
AGE:	21
OCCUPATION:	Counterman
CRIME:	Held up deli, shot owner Gustave Winkelmann, night
ACCOMPLICES:	Richard Mills, Arnold Sims 104–777
CLAIMS:	Was at home at the time of crime—denies guilt
JUDGE:	Goldstein, Kings County Court
SENTENCED:	4–22–46
RECEIVED:	4–22–46
EXECUTED:	7–10–47

7–5–46

Dear Mother

Before you come up Sunday, call the lawyer and bring him up with you. And when you come up stop and see the Warden, W E Snyder. I had a fight with two officers but I am all right now.

104778 Edward N Jones
219 St. James, Pl
Brooklyn NY

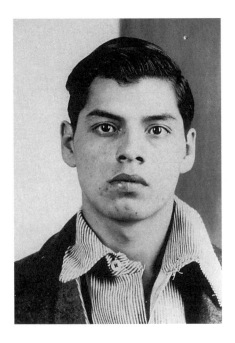

NAME: Harley LaMarr
NUMBER: 109–333
RACE: "Red" [Native American]
BORN: 9–25–30 (Buffalo)
AGE: 19
PHYSICAL: 5'11-½", 137 lbs.
RESIDENCE: Buffalo
KIN: Foster mother
EDUCATION: 8th grade
OCCUPATION: Laborer
CRIME: Shot Marion L. Frisbee with rifle
              in attempted rape, robbery, night
MOTIVE: No cause—needed money
ARESTED: 2–13–50
JUDGE: Munson, Erie County Court
SENTENCED: 4–17–50
RECEIVED: 4–17–50
EXECUTED: 1–11–51

Time: 10:00 p.m.
Place: Home
Date: April 19

Dear Harley:

You probably have received many letters from Buffalo in the past two weeks. It is only natural that we should feel closer to a person of our own age. One thing that has bothered me since I saw you at the Erie County Court House. You put on a good act that convinced most people that you were tough and not afraid. But when I saw you I knew that you were as afraid as any other person in your position. I can truly say that I believe the sentence was a big mistake. It seems that every time I pick up a newspaper that I see of a murder, but do they ever sentence these men and women to die? I haven't seen it happen yet. They wait till a boy of 19 makes a mistake till they decide that justice has to be done. This letter will be read before it gets to you (if it ever does) and I hope that the one who reads it will have mercy on you. It was brought up at the trial that you had no friends. Maybe you had none then but I am sure that you have now. Not only girls but boys too.

"God Bless You"
A Friend

Translation of letter in German from Baden, Germany, addressed to "Sing-Sing, U.S.A., Kommandant," no date:

I hold the Commandant and the guard unit fully and entirely responsible for the safety of the accused, Julius and Ethel Rosenberg.

Postcard to Warden, Sing Sing Prison, postmarked April 6, 1951, from Durham, New Hampshire:

Dear Sir:

Would you please forward this card to the proper authority. It is in the confirmed belief of an average American citizen. The people who will allow Julius & Ethel Rosenberg to live after they have been sentenced to death for a crime resulting in 60,000 American casualties (20,000 of them DEAD) are as guilty of contributing to those dead as the Rosenbergs themselves. This is still a free country and I'm expressing an opinion.
They should die as sentenced!

Sheldon Prescott, Durham, N.H.

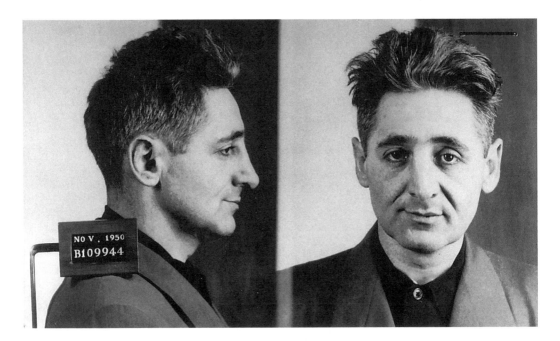

NAME: Bernard Stein
NUMBER: 109–944
AGE: 34
OCCUPATION: Bartender
MARITAL: Separated, 1 child
PHYSICAL: 5'9-¾", 151 lbs.
RESIDENCE: Chicago
CRIME: Shot Sol Moss, Mayfair Grill,
                   night, 7–10–46
ACCOMPLICES: John Reilly, Milton Shaket
CLAIMS: Claims innocence
JUDGE: Donnellan, New York Court
                   of General Sessions
SENTENCED: 11–6–50
RECEIVED: 11–6–50
EXECUTED: 3–6–52

Dear Warden:

From the week of February 3—Bernard Stein will go to the chair as the newspaper mentioned. This man is 34 years old, I feel bad for any youth going to his death. Try to make his little time somehow to have a little value—be not hard with him. Somehow I know you are human. The reason I took time to write this is because I feel bad for broken people like Stein he is so young and must die so early. The prison priest understands this situation—so warden guess I was compelled to write the words down where human feelings are concerned. I know warden you are a man with a proud position so I don't want to take up more of your precious time so I will come now to a polite close.

Devotedly,
Frederick

Hon. Robert J. Kirby,
Warden,
Institution.

Dear Sir:

On this date, at 1:20 pm, I was called to the
Condemned Cells to attend Dominick Sileo, father of Inmate #100,164, Sileo, for a contusion and slight lacera-
tion of the terminal end of the second finger, right
hand. Sterile dressing was applied.

Sileo states that while he was in the toilet,
with the door ajar, his daughter closed same, catching his
finger between the door and the jamb.

Very truly yours,

M. L. Moroney, R. N.

Copy to:
Dr. J.A.Kearney.
Moroney.

NAME:	Edmund Sileo aka William Hague
NUMBER:	100–664
AGE:	27
OCCUPATION:	Bookmaker
PHYSICAL:	5'10-¼', 127 lbs.
EDUCATION:	2 yrs. college
CRIME:	Shot and killed 2 men in bar and grille, night, automatic pistol, 8–3–40
CLAIMS:	Claims innocence
SENTENCED:	2–2–42
RECEIVED:	2–6–42
EXECUTED:	1–14–43

NAME:	Anthony Papa
NUMBER:	106–433
AGE:	27
OCCUPATION:	Button maker
MARITAL:	Married, 1 child
PHYSICAL:	5'8", 183 lbs.
CRIME:	Saw 5-year-old girl at his wedding, was attracted to her, struck and killed her, night, premises, Mineola, 4–19–47
CLAIMS:	Doesn't remember doing it (if he did it)
JUDGE:	Collins, Nassau County Court
SENTENCED:	10–22–47
RECEIVED:	10–22–47
EXECUTED:	7–1–48

Date May 29, 1945

I, ANTHONY R. PAPA, hereby request that, in the event that I am executed, my eyes be immediately removed and given to the New York Eye Bank, for whatever disposition and use they may wish.

Anthony R. Papa

I approve of the above gift.

Frances Papa
Wife

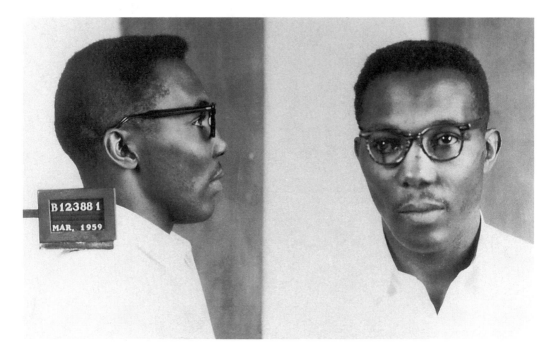

NAME:	Henry Flakes aka Snow Flakes
NUMBER:	123–881
BORN:	Alabama
AGE:	32
OCCUPATION:	Auto mechanic
HABITS:	Uses drugs
CRIME:	Killed Freedman in robbery
ACCOMPLICES:	Walter Green 123–880 and DeWitt Lee
JUDGE:	Jacob A. Latona, Erie County Court
SENTENCED:	3–6–59
RECEIVED:	3–7–59
EXECUTED:	5–19–60

NAME: Harry Epstein aka Hyman Epstein
NUMBER: 101–393
BORN: Russia
AGE: 47
OCCUPATION: Pocketbook maker
CRIME: Killed man with lead pipe
SENTENCED: 7–30–42
RECEIVED: 7–30–42
EXECUTED: Reversed judgment 3–18–43

1/25/57

Dear Warden:

I have talked to the other inmates and they have agreed that if the lights were left on all night it would not bother them.

The new spot lights which you were kind enough to install shines directly into the one cell, therefore would not bother anyone else.

At the present time some of us are doing some very urgent legal work and find it is much easier to concentrate at night because there is no noise at that time.

Very respectfully yours,
Elmer Burke 118–395

A week later Burke filed a lawsuit against Warden Denno and others. He was executed on January 9, 1958.

Cases

Even after they had been convicted and sentenced to death, many convicts worked unceasingly on their cases—pressing their lawyers, developing their appeals, or desperately combing their legal papers for some shred of exculpatory evidence that might help overturn their convictions or stall their executions. Most condemned persons had little formal education, and none had ever attended law school, yet some managed to acquire enough legal expertise to aid their cause—at least, for a while. Very few had the benefit of top lawyers working on their behalf, but some of those representing the inmates spared no effort to save their clients. In all, about one-third of those admitted to the Sing Sing Death House ultimately left it alive, usually to spend many more years in prison.

NAME: Ward Caraway
NUMBER: 105–407
AGE: 22
OCCUPATION: Chauffeur
HABITS: Marijuana
CRIME: Shot Marjorie Church Logan
                 in her home in robbery
CLAIMS: Drugs
JUDGE: Collins, Nassau County
SENTENCED: 12–18–46
RECEIVED: 12–18–46
EXECUTED: 7–3–47

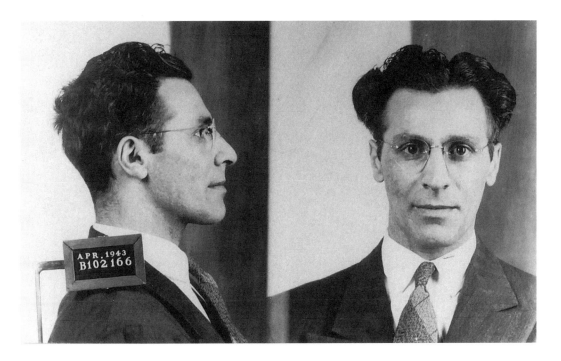

NAME:	Joseph Charles Mascari
	aka Joseph Charles Patane
NUMBER:	102–166
AGE:	31
OCCUPATION:	Delivery driver
CRIME:	Killed Rose O'Connell with hammer
JUDGE:	William H. Coon, Madison County
SENTENCED:	4–3–43
RECEIVED:	4–3–43
EXECUTED:	1–6–44

NAME: George Donaldson aka
                  Harry Doremus,
                  Edward Bedell,
                  Wm. Hazelhurst, Geo.
                  Hazelhurst, Wood-
                  chuck, George Wash-
                  ington
                  Donaldson

NUMBER: 104–139
BORN: Modena, NY
AGE: 48
OCCUPATION: Handyman
EDUCATION: 3rd grade
CRIME: Killed Edward Simp-
                  kins with crowbar at
                  Harlem Valley
                  Psychiatric Institute
RAP SHEET: Extensive criminal
                  history
KIN: No one
JUDGE: Clinton, Rensselaer
                  County
SENTENCED: 6–25–45
RECEIVED: 6–25–45
EXECUTED: 3–7–46

NAME: Webster Daniel
NUMBER: 105–546
AGE: 36
CRIME: Shot Patrolman
                  George Hunter while
                  fleeing from robbery
                  after drunken spree,
                  10–10–46
EXECUTED: 8–21–47

NAME:	Wallace Ford, Jr.
NUMBER:	111–433
BORN:	Montgomery, Alabama
AGE:	30
MARITAL:	Married, 2 children
PHYSICAL:	5'11", 150 lbs.
CRIME:	Hit sister-in-law, Nancy Bridges, ran her over with auto
CLAIMS:	Doesn't know why he did it
JUDGE:	Hamilton Ward, State Supreme Court, Genessee County
SENTENCED:	12–4–51
RECEIVED:	12–4–51
EXECUTED:	10–30–52

From a letter to Hon. John T. Loughran, Chief Justice,
New York State Court of Appeals, from Wallace Ford, Jr.

My attorneys at the trial were appointed by the Genesee County Court and they also represented me on appeal before this Court. I sincerely do believe that to the limit of their knowledge, capabilities and experience, they faithfully and conscientiously did their collective best and utmost to protect my interest. However, Your Honor, they were both young men, comparatively young in their practice of law and for both my case was the first murder trial and appeal.

November 23, 1953

Maurice O'Dell #113–865
Institution

Dear Sir:

I am sorry to inform you that I am in receipt of an Order of the Court of Appeals, fixing the week of January 4, 1954, as the date for carrying into effect the original sentence of death in your case.

Very truly yours,
/S/
Warden

NAME:	Maurice O'Dell aka Digger
NUMBER:	113–865
AGE:	28
OCCUPATION:	Waiter
MARITAL:	Single
PHYSICAL:	5'6", 134 lbs.
EDUCATION:	2 yrs. HS
HABITS:	Drug user
RESIDENCE:	Hamilton, Ontario
CRIME:	Shot Donald Hurd in jewelry store robbery
ACCOMPLICES:	Ralph Grubisch, Walter Griffen
CLAIMS:	Claims innocence
JUDGE:	Munson, State Supreme, Erie County
SENTENCED:	5–1–53
RECEIVED:	5–2–53
EXECUTED:	1–7–54

NAME:	Willard Phillips
NUMBER:	123–182
RACE:	Black
AGE:	42
OCCUPATION:	Laborer
MARITAL:	Divorced, 3 children
PHYSICAL:	5'6-¼", 136 lbs.
EDUCATION:	HS graduate
CRIME:	While committing rape, suffocated Sunday Graham, 8-year-old stepdaughter of his ex-wife
RAP SHEET:	Previous sex offender in Nassau County
CLAIMS:	Stupidity—ignorance
RESIDENCE:	Hempstead, Long Island
JUDGE:	Widlitz, Nassau County Court
SENTENCED:	10–17–58
RECEIVED:	10–17–58
EXECUTED:	6–23–60

*From His Legal Brief to the Supreme Court of the
United States of America*

Phillips spent the next 23 hours in police custody without being arraigned. He steadfastly maintained innocence for over 18 hours, confessing for the first time shortly after 5:00 a.m., May 14, 1958. During those 18 hours he was persistently questioned, had no food or drink and was without friendly advice or legal counsel. He was subjected to humiliating treatment by the police, confronted by the victim's stepmother and uncle, and was accorded no opportunity to lie down and sleep although he had risen at 6:15 a.m. on May 13th, was sleepy, and dozed occasionally while seated in a chair.

NIGHTLETTER
Hon. Governor Averill Harriman
Executive Mansion
Albany, N.Y.

Honorable Sir:

I am sentenced to die on Thursday, June 28. Please grant me a temporary respite for the following reasons. There is evidence that has not been presented that would prove my innocence. I was convicted on perjured testimony by the policemen and I have evidence that their testimony was perjury. I am physically unable to have committed the crime that I was accused of and can prove it. Please appoint an investigating committee under the Moreland Act for this case. I am innocent.

Ernest Lee Edwards
#117231

NAME:	Ernest Lee Edwards aka Carolina
NUMBER:	117–231
AGE:	21
OCCUPATION:	Counterman at White Tower
PHYSICAL:	5'11-¼", 148 lbs.
CRIME:	Struck Stanley Englander w/pipe, 7–5–54
ACCOMPLICE:	Richard F. Connors
CLAIMS:	Wasn't at the scene of the crime
JUDGE:	Liebowitz, Kings County Court
SENTENCED:	4–4–55
RECEIVED:	4–13–55
EXECUTED:	6–28–56

NEW YORK CITY
JUNE 28, 1956

GOVERNOR'S OFFICE HAS JUST ADVISED BY TELEPHONE NO FURTHER CONSID-
ERATION WILL BE GIVEN YOUR CASE. JUSTICE HARLAN IN DENYING STAY REN-
DERED LENGTHY OPINION RECEIVED TOO LATE TO SEND YOU. IN IT HE
ACKNOWLEDGES FOUR FEDERAL QUESTIONS HAD BEEN PRESENTED AND VIG-
OROUSLY PRESSED.

  1. PREJUDICIAL NEWSPAPER PUBLICITY ON INSPECTION OF SCENE.
  2. LIEBOWITZ'S REMARKS TO JURY CONCERNING APPELLATE REVIEW.
  3. LIEBOWITZ'S ALLEGED BIAS.
  4. CONNORS ALLEGED PERJURY.

HARLAN STATED HE DENIED STAY BECAUSE CONVINCED VOTE OF FOUR JUS-
TICES, MINIMUM ESSENTIAL TO GRANTING OF CERTIORARI, COULD NOT BE
OBTAINED IN YOUR FAVOR ON FOREGOING QUESTIONS. HIS OPINION EXPRESSLY
STATES WE HAVE DONE THE UTMOST FOR YOU. WE PROFOUNDLY REGRET NO
FURTHER JUDICIAL OR EXECUTIVE STEPS POSSIBLE.

JOHN F. FINERTY
CURTIS McCLANE

Clemency

Many of those who cheated the chair were spared by virtue of executive clemency. From 1935 to 1963, 249 convicts were executed but 72 had their death sentences commuted by the governor. At least one governor, Herbert Lehman, instituted a policy of automatically commuting an offender's punishment to life imprisonment if any judge on the Court of Appeals had voted to overturn the death sentence. But Buchalter of Murder, Inc. was not so lucky: although three of the seven judges dissented, Governor Dewey still denied him executive clemency, just as he would also reject the clemency plea of mother-of-five Helen Fowler. Some lawyers specialized in clemency bids, urging their clients to stop claiming innocence and to admit their guilt, hoping for a governor's mercy. Sometimes it worked, but usually it did not.

NAME:	Helen Ray Fowler
NUMBER:	102–981
AGE:	37
PHYSICAL:	5'7", 227 lbs.
KIN:	Widowed, 5 children
RESIDENCE:	Niagara Falls
OCCUPATION:	Housewife, rooming house
CRIME:	Beat husband, threw body in river, 2–11–44
ACCOMPLICE:	George F. Knight 102–982
CLAIMS:	Denies she killed him
JUDGE:	Munson, State Supreme Court, Niagara County
SENTENCED:	2–19–44
RECEIVED:	2–21–44
FILED APPEAL:	3–28–44
APPEALS ACTION:	Receipt of order of Court, 7–20–44, fixing date of execution for 9–4–44
RESPITE/STAY:	9–1–44, postponing execution date until wk. beginning 10–2–44; second respite on 10–4–44, postponing execution until wk. beginning 11-13-44
CLEMENCY:	No
EXECUTED:	11–16–44

file 102981

Lt. Governor Hanley,
Albany, N. Y.

Dear Governor:

         I had these things on my mind at the time of the trial. I hate the
disgrace of bringing these things out. I knew at the time of the trial Genevieve
would not do to be trusted because she wanted to be free so bad. She had ran away
five times, each time the officers were called. Once a fellow was prosecuted over
her running away and being with him in place of going to school. Another time she
told Andrew I wanted to borrow $30.00 was at the station in Niagara Falls. When I
caught her police were looking for her then. Genevieve and Neta Ventise were
picked up in Buffalo and held at my mother's request until we went for them. Once
I reported her missing and she knew I had notified the police so she went to a
hospital, had a squad car to bring her home. Said she was sick. Her and my daughter
Ruth both poisoned my husband and I to get rid of me. Ruth was going with my husband.
I have proof by Niagara Falls Police Department because of his arrest. I have a letter here to prove my husband went with one daughter. The other one just wanted to be
free. I can prove this. She lied on me just to get her freedom. She could have been
afraid as she said to a certain extent but what's been said since I have been in
trouble makes me know as I pray to have the chance to prove that she was trying to
get rid of me. I have a letter here to prove what I&m saying. She said she was free
for the first time in her life and intended to stay free. She also said I'd make a
nice fat crackling in the chair. She wanted freedom, she went directly from the
jail with $84.00 on her and went to living with a man &nd still is on that same day.
I have a letter here from one daughter threatening to help to prosecute me on assault
case and saying Jen and the other children would have their freedom then. I have an
undertakers bill of a subpoena for a bill of burying a child that belonged to my husband. Ruth would not even sign the petition for my life. When the two large girls
poisoned me I was to get away from home to go to Illinois. Their father had died
they said. If I was dead they could go to Illinois so they poisoned myself and husband and ran away but come back. Alarm was turned in then. I can prove this by a
Child Welfare Woman. I reported it to scare them right in front of them. Genevieve
and Ruth both hated me on account of G. Also because we did not work and they did.
Thats why Ruth ran away. She said so in her letter I have here. We gambled but they
did not like the idea. We quarr&led all the time over that. I&d put him out, he'd
kick the door in come back. Gen really could not sleep and working. She has started
and walked a block from home at three or four o'clock in the morning to try to find
a police because she could not sleep when he came in drunk.

         Governor, I was a good mother to my children. I washed, ironed, kept
roomers, boarders for their living. I was also on relief because there was some of
the children I had to support or their father would want to take them. So I supported them and a grand-child which is Ruth's and is living now but they have taken
her from her mother. I fought hard all the time to keep my children under a roof
with me. Please give me a chance to prove these things. I've said I&m not guilty
of any murder or robbery but I did help to get the man out of the house or he'd
have left him there in the trunk because he was drunk for over a week after and a
couple of days before. Please have mercy on me. Please spare my life. I&ve not
been no nuisance to society. I always did the best I could until I had to call in
an officer but I was scared to death over this. I never was around a thing like
this. The first thing you think of is your children. No one to keep them. I have
a little boy, ten, one five, a girl of fourteen, one, eighteen, one twenty, a grand-
child, I cared for all the time. I made a mistake by not calling the police because
I knew I'd be held and kept from my children. Please spare my life.

---2---

I did wrong, but please for God's sake, give me a chance to prove these things, and you'll see the things just like I do and not lying for my life and begging a chance to prove these things. I can. Please, I know you can if you please would. I never told my lawyer these things to bring out. Besides, I could not hear through the trial hardly anything that was said. I was deaf on one side. I have a doctor at Lockport to prove this. There is a lot of things that were said I never knew until I saw the court minutes. I kept asking the matron what was said. I never heard none of the children's statements clear at all. Just parts but I heard what lawyers and district attorneys said. I could not understand what the judge said. I know it's a late time to ask this to be done but I'm telling the truth and it can be proved so please help me. A life is a life and I'm framed through my own daughters just to be rid of me but as far as Knight he was afraid I'd tell on him because I threatened to. Please don't take my life until I have a chance to prove these things. I did not explain these things to my lawyer but he knew a few things but not these but I'm begging please let me prove this. If you'll please let my life be spared I'll tell you just where and how I can prove these things and through my lawyer. Please help me, please don't let me down for sticking to my children you see it's true or I'd have brought this out before now. It's a mother's love and it's been so much disgrace but this is the truth of why I am here. Please I'll live for God from now on if spared for when children try to have your life taken just to be free, it's a shame. I was awful hard on them about taverns, clubs, cars which I thought was right.

_8.30 P.m._

Westchester County, New York
Sworn to before me this _16th_
day of November 1944.

Helen Fowler

John J. McCue
Notary Public

This statement was phoned to Mr Chas Breitel and also called to the attention of Acting Governor Joseph Hanley at about 9.40 P.M. Nov 16, 1944

W. E. Snyder

Escape Attempts

Although Sing Sing's death house was billed as the world's most escape-proof prison, that didn't keep some convicts from hatching elaborate escape plans and trying to carry them out. Prison authorities took extraordinary security precautions to discourage any action that might enhance an inmate's ability to slip away. Overheard conversations and intercepted notes were routed to the principal keeper, and frequent cell searches occasionally turned up suspicious or dangerous objects, such as drawings and weapons. At least one apparent conspiracy involved a plan to kidnap the warden's family to use as hostages in order to free several convicts on death row. But the death house withstood every threat. From the time it opened in 1922 to the day it closed in 1969, nobody escaped.

SURVEILLANCE NOTES TO THE PRINCIPAL KEEPER

Mr. L. J. Kelley
Principal Keeper
Inst.

Dear Sir:

In re: to Salemi's visit as of this date, the conversation between this inmate and his visitor Rose Perillo was in the Italian language—for an approximate period of about 45 minutes.

Respectfully
J. J. McGoey
C.C. in chg.
4–8–55

April 8, 1955

Part of conversation that took place between Salemi #114193 and his visit Rose Parillo on Friday, April 8, 1955:

Rose Parillo: What way do they take you to Court?
Salemi: We will probably go down through Tarrytown late Monday.
Rose Parillo: Is that the Warden's car you go in?
Salemi: I think it is.
Rose Parillo: What does he do, walk to work when you have the use of the car?
Salemi: No, he probably has another car that he uses. You know we also have an escort of State Troopers.
Rose Parillo: Where do they park the car down at the Court House?
Salemi: I don't know.

The conversation then returned to the Court witnesses and Judge Goldstein.

Respectfully yours,
R. Ward
2:30 pm to 10:30 pm

April 9, 1955

Mr. Louis J. Kelley
Principal Keeper

Dear Sir:

In reference to Salemi's #114-193 visit with brothers Joseph and Nicholas Salemi: A large part of the conversation was in the Italian language. What English was spoken concerned the case. Witnesses Judge Goldstein and relatives.

Respectfully yours,
R. Ward

4-9-55

Data on Salemi visit with 2 Brothers Nicholas & Joseph Salemi.
1st 30 minutes conversation in Italian language subdued tones just above whispering.
2nd conversation in English same in re: to case.
3rd Brother Joseph taking notes in English same in re: to case.
4th duration of note writing 45 minutes: 2:30 pm end of my tour.

J. J. McGoey
CC In chge
4-9-55

April 10, 1955

Mr. L. Kelley
Principal Keeper

Dear Sir

This is to inform you that on April 9th, 1955 at approximately 3:40 p.m. as per your instructions I ask both Joseph and Nicholas Salemi if they would show me the note that they had written while visiting with their brother Leonardo who is in the condemn cells. Both denied having written anything. When ask by me if they would volunteer to a frisk Joseph volunteered but Nicholas shook his head no. I then told him that he would be searched if he didn't voluntarily hand over any writing that he had taken. He then reached into his pocket and took out two pages of notes that he admitted writing while visiting with Leonardo. I ask him why he took the notes and his reply was that he had noticed other visitors taking notes. The notes that Nicholas had written were read to you over the phone.

Respectfully,
Sgt. W. Byrne

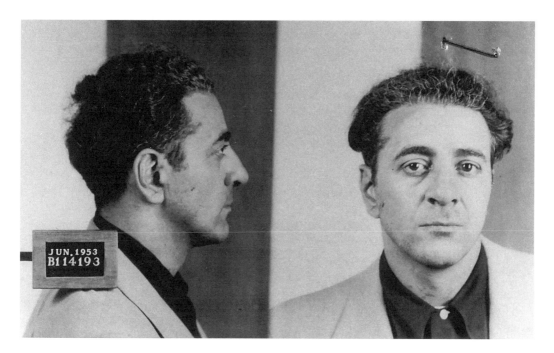

NAME:	Leonardo Salemi
NUMBER:	114–193
AGE:	41
OCCUPATION:	Plasterer
PHYSICAL:	5'5", 135 lbs.
CRIME:	Shot Walter Forlenza, bar, night
RAP SHEET:	Very extensive criminal history
CLAIMS:	Completely innocent of this particular murder
JUDGE:	Jonah Goldstein, NY General Sessions
SENTENCED:	6–24–53
RECEIVED:	6–24–53
EXECUTED:	2–28–57

Kite confiscated from Rosario:

It is impossible to get any guns in here and we have to have guns to get away. What we are planning to do is to have the wardens home taken over and him used as a tool to bring my boy in with him as a visiting cop. He will have the stuff with him and we use the wardens family as hostages. It only take 2 or 3 men outside and I have boy out there who knows the whole plan with the times and all the details. Are you in? Its better than waiting around to just die like sheep. What can we lose?
TEAR UP AND FLUSH IN TOILET!

NAME: Romulo Rosario
NUMBER: 115–664
BORN: Rio Piedras, PR, 7–6–16
                (naturalized)

AGE: 37
MARITAL: Married, 2 children
PHYSICAL: 5'7-½", 198 lbs.
CRIME: Shot Michael Gonzalez, street, day
CLAIMS: Self-defense
JUDGE: Saul S. Streit, NY Court of Gen-
                eral Sessions

SENTENCED: 5–14–54
RECEIVED: 5–14–54
EXECUTED: 2–17–55

NAME:	Gerhard Puff aka Donald Jardine, Richard Rogers
NUMBER:	113–970
BORN:	2–13–14 (Dresden, Germany)
AGE:	39
OCCUPATION:	Truck driver
PHYSICAL:	5'11-¼", 165 lbs.
EDUCATION:	8th grade
NEXT OF KIN:	Wife (in prison)
CRIME:	Shot and killed Joseph J. Brock, FBI agent, in Congress Hotel while on lam from bank robbery
CLAIMS:	Shot in self-defense
JUDGE:	Sylvester J. Ryan, U.S. District Court
SENTENCED:	5–15–53
RECEIVED:	5–20–53
EXECUTED:	8–12–54

P.S. 280—1C-22

INTER-DEPARTMENTAL COMMUNICATION

December 4, 1953

Hon. W. L. Denno
Warden

Dear Sir:

Attached please find a diagram of keys, found in the cell of Gerhard Puff, #113-970, at the Condemned Cells.

This diagram was shown to the 6:30 AM to 2:30 PM, 2:30 PM to 10:30 PM and 10:30 PM to 6:20 AM shifts and warned of the carelessness of handling of keys and shown what can be done when certain inmates are capable of designing same.

Yours very truly,

L. J. Kelley
Principal Keeper

LJK:p
encls.

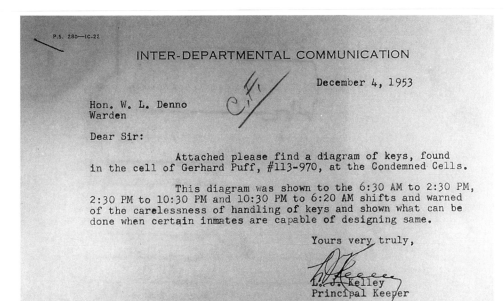

CLASS OF SERVICE

This is a full-rate
Telegram or Cable-
gram unless its de-
ferred character is in-
dicated by a suitable
symbol above or pre-
ceding the address.

WESTERN UNION

1201

W. P. MARSHALL, PRESIDENT

SYMBOLS

DL = Day Letter

NL = Night Letter

LC = Deferred Cable

NLT = Cable Night Letter

Ship Radiogram

The filing time shown in the date line on telegrams and day letters is STANDARD TIME at point of origin. Time of receipt is STANDARD TIME at point of destination

=SYB095

SY-NC 628 PD=NJA NEWYORK NY 8 607P=

WARDEN SING SING PRISON

NEW YORK=OSSINING NY=

STAY ALL EXECUTIONS TONIGHT=

ARC=

COMPANY WILL APPRECIATE SUGGESTIONS FROM ITS PATRONS CONCERNING ITS SERVICE

Stay

Pending a successful appeal, a finding of insanity, or clemency, the most an inmate could hope for was to receive a temporary stay or respite from the governor, delaying the scheduled execution. Without it, nothing would stop the clock from reaching its fatal destination. In the waning hours, prisoners and wardens alike nervously awaited a last-minute reprieve. Sometimes word arrived by telegraph or telephone, announcing either that hope was lost or that the execution was postponed.

NAME: Emile Scott
NUMBER: 114–658
AGE: 20
PHYSICAL: 6'1", 183 lbs.
OCCUPATION: Builder
MARITAL: Married, 2 children
CRIME: Shot Patrolman
               John L. Pendergrass,
               street, night
CLAIMS: Merely an innocent
               bystander
JUDGE: Streit, New York
               Court of General
               Sessions
SENTENCED: 10–30–53
RECEIVED: 10–30–53
EXECUTED: 7–15–54

June 28, 1954

Dear Mother:

. . . As it stands now it looks like I got 6 lawyers and getting a seventh. . . . I've told you time and time again that the stay is the most important thing. Going back to the court of Appeals is nothing compared to the stay. . . .

Your loving son
Emile H. Scott
114658CC

NAME:	Julio Perez
NUMBER:	107–645
BORN:	Ponce, PR
AGE:	36
OCCUPATION:	Laborer
PHYSICAL:	5'6-¾", 142 lbs.
CRIME:	Stabbed w/screw-driver and strangled Vera Lotito, day
JUDGE:	Donnellan, New York General Sessions
SENTENCED:	11–23–48
RECEIVED:	11–23–48
EXECUTED:	5–25–50

WESTERN UNION
--SYMO45
SY.CAA075 PD=CA ALBANY NY 334P

HON WILLIAM E SNYDER=
WARDEN SING SING PRISON OSSINING NY=

CONFIRMING OUR TELEPHONE CONVERSATION CLERK OF THE UNITED STATES SUPREME COURT ADVISES THAT STAY OF EXECUTION HAS BEEN ORDERED BY SAID COURT FOR JULIO RAMIREZ PEREZ. CERTIFIED COPY OF ORDER IS BEING MAILED BY CLERK OF SUPREME COURT=GEORGE M SHAPIRO ASSISTANT COUNSEL TO THE GOVERNOR.

NAME: Virgil Richardson
NUMBER: 120–833
AGE: 28
PHYSICAL: 5'5-½", 122 lbs.
OCCUPATION: Clerk
CRIME: Shot Patrolman William
                   G. Long, parking lot, as he
                   caught defendant tamper-
                   ing with car in parking lot
JUDGE: Impellitteri, Queens
                   County Court
SENTENCED: 5–3–57
RECEIVED: 5–3–57
EXECUTED: 11–20–58

WESTERN UNION

MRS M RICHARDSON
456 MADISON ST
BROOKLYN 21, NY

DEAR MOM. RECEIVED
TWO WEEK STAY. SEE
YOU LATER.

YOUR SON
VIRGIL RICHARDSON
120833.

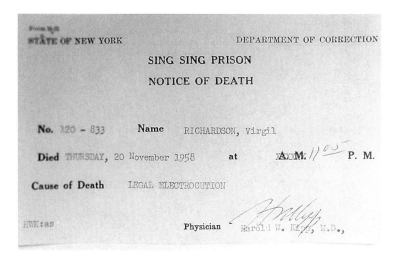

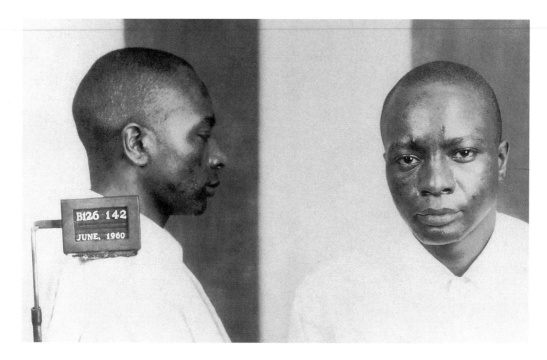

NAME:	Woodrow Miller
NUMBER:	126–142
HABITS:	User of cocaine, heroin, marijuana
CRIME:	Shot Joseph Graber in liquor store robbery, night
CLAIMS:	No reason given
ARRESTED:	11–27–57
MARITAL:	Separated, 2 children
JUDGE:	Samuel Liebowitz, Kings County Court
SENTENCED:	6–10–60
RECEIVED:	6–11–60
EXECUTED:	6–8–61

Newspaper clipping, 4–26–61:

His last appeal denied, twice-convicted killer Woodrow Miller, 33, formerly of 783 Prospect Place, Brooklyn, will die in the electric chair for the shotgun slaying of Joseph Graber, 31, who was the father of seven including quadruplets.

NAME:	Louis Parisi
NUMBER:	103–095
AGE:	24
MARITAL:	Single
CRIME:	Shot Vincent Roppa, night,
CLAIMS:	7–30–42
JUDGE:	Denies guilt
	Wallace, NY General Sessions
SENTENCED:	7–1–43
RECEIVED:	7–1–43
EXECUTED:	6–3–44

JUNE 4, 1944.

MR. W.E. SNYDER
WARDEN
INSTITUTION
103–095

DEAR SIR:

AT 12:53 AM MR. SABBATINO ATTORNEY FOR *PARISI* CALLED AND ASKED IF HE, PARISI, HAD BEEN EXECUTED. I INFORMED HIM THAT THE EXECUTION HAD TAKEN PLACE AS SCHEDULED.

RESPECTFULLY,
J.P. SULLIVAN, LIEUTENANT

From the New York Herald Tribune, *October 20, 1958:*

Slayer, Already Executed, Loses High Court Plea

WASHINGTON, DC. Oct. 19 (AP) — Ralph Dawkins, already exe-cuted, was the loser today in a Supreme Court order that didn't matter to him. Convicted of killing a South Ozone Park, Queens, N.Y., grocer in a 1957 holdup, Dawkins appealed to the high court and was turned down last April. He asked recon-sideration but filed to request a stay of execution and was put to death July 16. There was no official notification to the Supreme Court that the case had been disposed of with such finality when today it denied his request for a rehearing.

NAME:	Ralph Dawkins
NUMBER:	121–818
AGE:	20
OCCUPATION:	Waiter
MARITAL:	Married, 1 child
PHYSICAL:	5'10-½", 145 lbs.
CRIME:	Shot Wm. Boser w/pistol, robbery
ACCOMPLICES:	Jackson Turner 121–817,
	William A. Wynn 121–819,
	Thomas Frye 121–820
CLAIMS:	Self-defense
JUDGE:	McGrattan, Queens County Court
SENTENCED:	12–27–57
RECEIVED:	12–27–57
EXECUTED:	7–16–59

July 5, 1953

Warden Denno

Dear Sir,

I would like to ask a favor from you. I have only 11 days left. I would like to move to some where, where it is quiet.

I have some letter to write and with the noise on the East Wing I cant think right. I do not want to cause trouble for the boys. But I would like to move some where. Where I could write my letter.

I hope and pray that you will be able to help me in this matter. Thanking you Sir for the time and consideration you will give this matter.

Sincerely,
112748CC

The Letter

When all hope was finally exhausted and the end was near, the condemned man or woman often spent some private moments composing a personal letter to a loved one. For many, it was a spiritual rite as much as a psychological necessity. Wherever such letters exist they convey, perhaps better than anything else, the writer's mental and emotional state—his or her core beliefs and feelings. Some letters were intended to heal a raging wound; others expressed remorse or contempt for past wrongs. A few tried to make sense of seeming insanity or to explain the ways of the world. But none of the death house letters was delivered in time for the writer to receive a reply.

NAME:	Ivory Mason
NUMBER:	124–004
RACE:	Black
BORN:	2–15–19 (Charleston, SC)
OCCUPATION:	Janitor
RESIDENCE:	Memphis, Tennessee
MARITAL:	Married (bigamist)
PHYSICAL:	5'9", 155 lbs.
EDUCATION:	Never attended school; couldn't read or write when he arrived at the prison
CRIME:	Shot Marie Wingfall with pistol, 3–25–54
CLAIMS:	Claims innocence
SENTENCED:	4–7–59
RECEIVED:	4–7–59
EXECUTED:	1–14–60

1—14—60

Dear Mother:

Just a few lines to let you hear from me as this will be my last letter to you. . . .

There is not much to say. I must tarry on to my maker from which I come. But don't worry mother. I have made my peace with God. I've been so dispirited in this life that maybe the life to come will be peace and happiness. And don't worry about burying my body. Let the State take care of that just pray that all you know as I that we were not put here to stay forever. So we all must return one day. . . . And mother since you did not come to see me. I forgive you. I understand. . . . And remember I enjoyed all your letters and every thing you did for me sorry if I cause you any heart ache and pains if so please forgive me. So I will close and until we meet beyond the river it is well remembered I were your Son. So this will be my last letter to you. And may God forever bless and keep you in his care.

I will close.

Good bye
Your son
Ivory Mason
1 24—004

PS. Always remember I am a change man and I have prayed and ask forgiveness for my sins and for my God to take me home.

Letter to Vincent Dermody,
Manhattan assistant district attorney,
the prosecutor who won
Leonard Salemi's death sentence:

Date: Feb. 25, 1957
Special Delivery

Dear Mr. Dermody:

I know this letter will come as a surprise to you . . . the last guy in the world you expect to hear from is me—Leonard Salemi! . . .

Anyway, since it appears that its all over but the shouting now I am sending you a little momento, which I highly prized and valued here! Something which I hope you will be big enough to accept in the good spirit and intent which they are meant. . . . They are my own hand made, molded I should say—Rosary beads. They are made of "Bread" Vince and no doubt the only ones of their kind in the world! Bread as you know is our secret commune with our beloved Lord Jesus Christ who died on the cross forgiving his executioners. They are as durable as any others and the pierced sacred heart and decades were colored in red by adding a small amount of cherry cool aid concentrate into the bread which I worked into a doughy substance for molding purpose. There is also a small amount of sugar added to give the needed glucose which veritably turns the beads into stonelike substance when completely dried out. And please, Vince, even though I know that you know better, don't let the press know about this letter, or especially about the beads.

Goodbye Vince—if its not asking too much offer up a prayer for me sometime. Except for that one bitterness and hate, I go out in peace. I am

Sincerely and Respectfully Yours,
Leonard Salemi
114193

Letter to a Friend

Late Wed. Nite
"Time for Last Goodbyes."

And now it's time for last goodbyes
Goodbyes . . . without . . . any crys
Can't reach out to touch—or kiss
Your eyes are dimmed and your face reveals the
    sting.
Sorry, dear, for all your pain, and tears.
But try to recall the happy years.
One for the road . . . is an old byword.
Make mine a smile, for this last time.
And now, its time to go . . . farewell dear heart.
No . . . please dont cry . . . let a big smile be
    my guide.
For its time now . . . for last . . . goodbyes.

Your Buddy
Lennie 114193

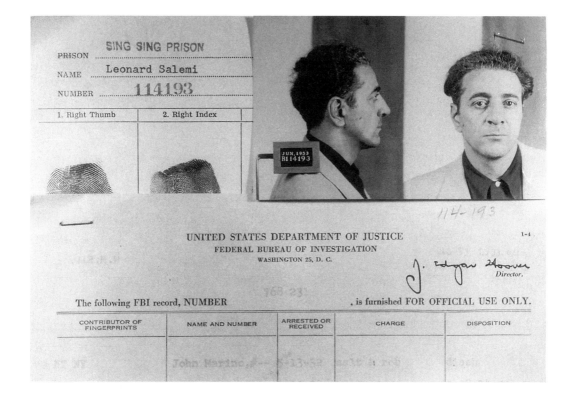

My dearest Friend:

I know what you are feeling at this moment. I am sure it is the same kind of feeling that my own family feels right now! I've seen their faces Sat. and felt their own pain with them. Long ago I foresaw their agony and unspoken suffering. And here is something else that may surprise you to hear, but as God is my judge, it is his own Gospel truth. As a boy, when my Dad was murdered cold bloodily while coming home from work with my brother Joey one night I actually "foresaw myself sitting in the electric chair!" I was only a kid of eleven years old then Sal—and of course I took an oath to avenge his killing! Shortly after I had seen a picture in one of our local scandle sheets—I believe it was the N.Y. Evening Graphic, of a person sitting in the electric chair. Well, Sal, I remembered that picture "and actually saw myself grown up and sitting in this same chair." I never dreamed however Sal, that one day I would for something that I had no part of! That's what really makes it hard. A guy don't give a damn when he goes out "knowing he was guilty."

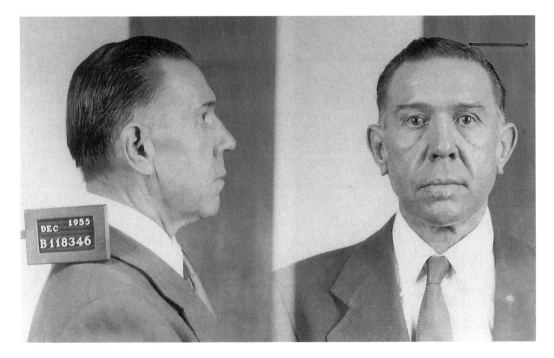

NAME:	Frank Newman
NUMBER:	118–346
AGE:	50
MARITAL:	Widower, 3 children
PHYSICAL:	5'6-½", 157 lbs.
EDUCATION:	8th grade
RELIGION:	Protestant
RESIDENCE:	Massapequa, Long Island
CRIME:	Shot wife Ethel, yard, day, 10–9–54
CLAIMS:	Temporary insanity—acute alcoholism
JUDGE:	Donohoe, Nassau County Court
SENTENCED:	12–2–55
RECEIVED:	12–2–55
EXECUTED:	8–23–56

August 22, 1956

Dear Junior
Dear Warren

It is so difficult for me to put in writing the sadness that is in my heart for you boys. . . .

I do want you to know that I have respect love and affection for you. Son, I could go on page after page but I do not believe I could describe how much I despise myself for this terrible thing. I loved Mother. I pray to God to forgive me and that my boys will try to soften the terrible hatred you have for me. . . .

May God guide and watch over you always.

Love
Dad
Frank Newman #118–346

Handwritten letter from Julius Rosenberg, 110–649, to his attorney, June 18, 1953:

Mr. Emanuel Block
401 Broadway
New York New York

Dear Manny:

I have drawn up a last will and testament so that there can be no question about the fact that I want you to handle our affairs and be responsible for the children as in fact you have been doing. Ethel completely concurs in this request and is in her own hand attesting to it.

Our children are the apple of our eye, our pride and most precious fortune, love them with all your heart and always protect them in order that they grow up to be normal healthy people. That you will do this I am sure, but as their proud father I take the prerogative to ask of you my dearest friend and devoted brother. I love my sons most profoundly.

I am not much at saying goodbyes because I believe that good accomplishments live on forever, but this I can say my love of life has never been so strong because I've seen how beautiful the future can be. Since I feel that we in some small measure have contributed our share in this direction. I think that my sons and millions of others will have benefited by it.

Words fail me when I attempt to tell of the nobility and grandeur of my life's companion, my sweet and devoted wife. Ours is a great love and a wonderful relationship, it has made my life full and rich.

My aged and ailing mother has been a source of great comfort and we always showed a mutual love and devotion. Indeed she has been selfless in her efforts in our behalf. My sisters and my brother have supported us from the start and were behind us 100% and worked on our behalf. We can truthfully say that my family gave us sustenance in our great trials.

You Manny are not only considered of my family but are our extra special friend. The bond of brotherhood and love between us was forged in the struggle for life and all that it means, and it is a source of great strength to us. Be strong for us beloved friend and we wish you long life to continue your fruitful work in health and happiness for without doubt you are a fine man, dear friend and sweet advocate of the people. I salute you and caress you affectionately with all my heart. *Never let them change the truth of our innocence.*

For peace, bread and roses in simple dignity we face the executioner with courage, confidence—never losing faith.

As ever,
Julie

P.S. All my personal effects are in three cartons and you can get them from the Warden. Ethel writes it is made known that we are the first victims of American Fascism.

Ethel & Julie
June 19, 1953

Dearest Manny,

The following letter is to be delivered to my children:

Dearest Sweethearts, my most precious children,

Only this morning it looked like we might be together again after all. Now that this cannot be, I want so much for you to know all that I have come to know. Unfortunately, I may write only a few simple words; the rest your own lives must teach you, even as mine taught me.

At first, of course, you will grieve bitterly for us but you will not grieve alone. That is our consolation and it must eventually be yours.

Eventually, too, you must come to believe that life is worth the living. Be comforted that even now, with the end of ours slowly approaching, that we know this with a conviction that defeats the executioner!

Your lives must teach you, too, that good cannot really flourish in the midst of evil; that freedom and all the things that go to make up a truly satisfying and worthwhile life, must sometimes be purchased very dearly. Be composed then, that we were serene and understood with the deepest kind of understanding, that civilization had not as yet progressed to the point where life did not have to be lost for the sake of life; and that we were comforted in the sure knowledge that others would carry on after us.

We wish we might have had the tremendous joy and gratification of living our lives out with you. Your Daddy who is with me in these last momentous hours sends his heart and all the love that is in it for his dearest boys. Always remember that we were innocent and could not wrong our conscience.

We press you close and kiss you with all our strength.

Lovingly
Daddy and Mommy—
Julie Ethel

P.S.—To Manny: The Ten Commandments, religious medal and chain—and my wedding ring—I wish you to present to our children as a token of our undying love—

P.S.—To Manny: Please be certain to give my best wishes to Saul Miller. Tell him I love and honor him with all my heart. Tell him I want him to know that I feel he shares my triumph— For I have no fear and no regrets—Only that the release from the trap was not completely effected and the qualities I possessed could not expand to their fullest capacities. I want him to have the pleasure of knowing how much he meant to me, how much he did to help me grow up. All our love to all our dear ones.

Love you so much.
Ethel

NAME:	Jauvhan Jackson
NUMBER:	105–850
AGE:	18
OCCUPATION:	Helper, rug dept.
PHYSICAL:	6'1-¼", 169 lbs.
CRIME:	Shot Leslie Hatter, holdup, day
ACCOMPLICE:	Matthew Wallace
CLAIMS:	Needed money
JUDGE:	S. S. Liebowitz, Kings County
SENTENCED:	4–7–47
RECEIVED:	4–7–47
EXECUTED:	1–9–48

Thursday

July 1, 1943

Mr. John J. Shanahan
Chief Engineer
Institution

Dear Sir:

This will inform you that there are three executions scheduled for Thursday, July 8, 1943.
Kindly make the usual arrangements.

Very truly yours,
/S/
WARDEN

Cairo, New York
June 14th 1953

Mr. W. L. Denno, Warden
Sing Sing Prison,
Ossining, New York.

Dear Warden Denno:

Your letter of June 12, 1953 informing me of two executions scheduled for Thursday, June 18, 1953 received.

I will report in the usual manner on that day.

Very truly yours,
Joseph P. Francel
[Rosenberg executioner]

December 23, 1958

Mr. W. L. Denno
Warden
Institution

Dear Warden Denno:

I am most grateful for your kindness in permitting the baptism of Leroy Keith, CC–#121–976, in the institutional chapel which took place this afternoon. I am sure that the impressive ceremony will make lasting impression upon this man because to date he has studied very faithfully and was well prepared for the reception of the sacrament.

With gratitude for your kindness and the men who carried out this detail in such an efficient and reverent way, I am

Sincerely yours
(Rev.) George F. McKinney
Catholic Chaplain

Warden Denno.
Assignments for executions scheduled for tonight—August 12, 1954

Lt. Toploski	-	leg electrode
Sgt. Tautenham	-	left side
Sgt. Werber	-	right "
Sgt. Goldfarb	-	Legs (ankle straps)
Sgt. Taylor	-	Dinner
P.K. Kelley	-	Usual

PRE-EXECUTION MEAL AS REQUESTED BY INMATE, MAY 19, 1960

Henry Flakes—#123–881

Dinner	Supper
Barbecued Chicken	Lobster
1 bottle Darby barbecued sauce	Lettuce & tomato salad w/olives and
French Fries	mayonnaise
Lettuce & tomato salad w/ripe olives and	Butter & rolls
mayonnaise	Ice Cream
Rolls and butter	1 box chocolate Candy
Strawberry Shortcake w/whipped cream	4 cigars (El Producto)
4 pkgs. Cigarettes	2 Pepsi Cola
Coffee, milk and sugar	Coffee, milk and sugar

The Chair

J. J. Shanahan, Chief Engineer, April 10, 1942:

The Control Equipment such as Voltage Regulators, Auto Transformers, Oil Circuit Breakers, Panel Board, etc., was designed by and supplied by General Electric Company. Prior to the Institution going to Alternating Current, a Consulting Engineer, Mr. G.M. Ogle aided the design of the Electric System. The design for the present system using the Institution supply of Alternating Current was by a Mr. H.M. Jalonack in 1931, an engineer employed by General Electric.

PARAMOUNT THEATRE
TIMES SQUARE
NEW YORK

OFFICE OF THE
MANAGING DIRECTOR

June 30, 1948

Acting Warden C. J. Ferling
Sing Sing Prison
Ossining, N.Y.

Dear Warden:

Thank you for your kind invitation to be present as a witness at the execution of Anthony R. Papa on July 1st.

Inasmuch as this letter did not reach me until the morning of the 30th, it was too late for me to arrange my appointments to be there in time.

However, please accept my sincere thanks for remembering to communicate with me.

Sincerely yours,
ROBERT M. WEITMAN

Witness

What makes someone request permission to witness an execution? What are the relationships between the condemned, the executioners, and the witnesses? The answers to these and other questions are often subject to speculation, yet they may help explain some essential aspects of capital punishment.

At Sing Sing, as in executions performed at the end of the twentieth century, the state required those present formally to attest and certify that they had witnessed the implementation of the death sentence. Some among the witnesses attended for the express purpose of reporting to the public about what had happened; others were required to attend, in the performance of their jobs.

Middletown Police Social Club
Middletown, New York
Incorporated 1919
Affiliated with Police Conference, State of New York

March 8, 1954

Warden W. L. Denno
Sing Sing Prison
Ossining, New York

Dear Sir:

This is to acknowledge your invitation to the executions on Thursday March 11, 1954. I am replying for Ptl. Edward Durkin and myself. We will both attend.

Respectfully yours,
Sherwood Myers

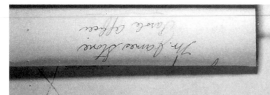

VICTORY EXTERMINATORS

General Extermination — No Binding Contracts

Telephones:
Mount Kisco 4080
After 6 P. M.
Gladstone 1677

TEN YEAR GUARANTEE
ON MOTHS

FIVE YEAR GUARANTEE
ON TERMITES

June 30, 1947

HARWOOD BUILDING
SCARSDALE, N. Y.
───
Telephone Scarsdale 6079

Wm. E. Snyder, Warden
Sing Sing Prison
Ossining, N.Y.

Dear Sir:-

    We, Frederick O. Wellington, Clarence Swicker
and Walter Jerman would like to be State Witnesses
for the state executions scheduled on or about
July 12, 1947.

    Each of us would greatly appriciate hearing
from you regarding our request.

                Very truly yours

                Frederick O. Wellington

FOW:W

    Frederick O. Wellington
    53 Bank Street
    White Plains, N.Y.

    Walter Jerman
    53 Bank Street
    White Plains, N.Y.

    Clarence Zwicker
    49 Bank Street
    White Plains, N.Y.

THE PEOPLE OF THE
STATE OF NEW YORK
AGAINST
JOHN RANFORD #102–682

I, *WILLIAM E. SNYDER* Warden of Sing Sing Prison, Pursuant to Section 508 of the Code of Criminal Procedure of the State of New York, do hereby certify that, in obedience thereto and in conformity with the judgment and sentence of the above Court, which judgment has been affirmed by the Court of Appeals of the State of New York, did attend on the *25th day of May 1944* at Sing Sing Prison, Ossining, Westchester County, New York, upon the execution of the judgment of said Court, and that the said *John Ranford* the prisoner named therein, was then and there, to wit, at the time and place aforesaid, executed in conformity with the provisions of the Code of Criminal Procedure of the State of New York.

I do further certify that the persons invited by me as such Warden, to be present at said execution, and whose names are hereinafter subscribed were the persons and all the persons present and witnessing the execution of judgment and sentence upon the said *JOHN RANFORD #102–682.*

. . . .
WARDEN OF SING SING PRISON

Dated, Ossining, N.Y.
May 25, 1944

We, the undersigned, do certify that we were present and witnessed the execution of the judgment and sentence of *JOHN RANFORD #102–684* as set forth in the foregoing certificate and we do hereby, pursuant to the Statute, at Sing Sing Prison, Ossining, Westchester County, New York, subscribed to the same on the *25th day of May, 1944.*

WITNESSES:	OFFICERS:
E. B. Ferguson	Thomas J. Keeley, *Principal Keeper*
I. Popps	Chas. W. Priest, *Asst. Prin. Keeper*
Emil B. Spivak	F. Vetter, *Captain*
D. A. Young	M. Darrow, *Sergeant*
Raymond Ayers	J. Nolan, *Sergeant*
Fred Morris	John A. Lamahan, *Sergeant*
Sanford Rivenburgh	Louis J. Kelley, *Lieutenant*
J. Woodrow Wilson	Wm. T. Alger, *Sgt.*
John M. Horn	Alfred G. Werben, *Sgt.*
George T. Griffen	J. Toploski, *Sgt.*
John E. Allen	
Julian B. Moss	
J. C. Dorbandt	
Robert H. Fillmore	
Robert I. Bennett	
Gustave Mederer	
Raymond Harrigan	
Hugo W. Busch	
Harold E. Pullen	

NAME: John Ranford
NUMBER: 102–682
AGE: 40
PHYSICAL: 6', 164 lbs.
EDUCATION: No schooling
RELIGION: Baptist
CRIME: Struck Valdemar E. Nielson with tire iron,
               robbery, day, Manhassett, LI
CLAIMS: Claims innocence
JUDGE: Collins, Nassau County Court
SENTENCED: 11–17–43
RECEIVED: 11–17–43
EXECUTED: 5–25–44

NAME:	Pablo Vargas
NUMBER:	123–636
BORN:	1–15–25
	(Puerto Rico)
AGE:	34
OCCUPATION:	Cook helper, Jewish Memorial Hosp.
MARITAL:	Married, 3 children
PHYSICAL:	5'9-½", 183 lbs.
EDUCATION:	8th grade
CRIME:	Choked and strangled Lillian Mojica, 2–13–58, set fire to house
CLAIMS:	Forced confession
JUDGE:	Geller, New York General Sessions
SENTENCED:	12–18–58
RECEIVED:	1–23–59
EXECUTED:	5–12–60

May 12, 1960

Mr. W. J. Denno
Warden

Dear Sir:

The wording on the sign carried by the two pickets read as follows—Thou shalt not kill on one side and clemency for Pablo Vargas—Vigil for His Life on the other side. On the other sign is Death Penalty is legalized murder—Catholic Workers 39 Spring N.Y.C. and on the other side is Clemency for Pablo Vagras Join the Vigil for His Life at Sing Sing.

Sgt. Byrne

From the Associated Press, May 13, 1960:

Prison authorities said it was the first time in more than 600 executions at Sing Sing since 1891 that a doomed man physically fought to the last moment to prevent his execution.

Resistance

From Warden Denno's letter to Commissioner Paul D. McGinnis,
May 17, 1960:

RE: Pablo Vargas, #123–636

Dear Commissioner:

. . . I wish to advise that it was anticipated that Vargas might pull some stunt due to the fact that his wife and other relatives were driven to this institution by a representative of a Spanish newspaper in New York City, and when the visit was completed the same newspaper man picked up the relatives in their car. It is also my understanding that one of the newspapers paid the expenses of attorney Nancy Carley to go to Washington to try to get a stay of execution. It would appear that apparently this inmate was reassured that he would get a stay of execution, and when this did not come through he became very upset. As a matter of fact, he showed signs of getting jittery right after his wife, sister and half-brother left the institution. Therefore, I had some extra officers out of sight in the event that he did something unusual. He walked into the execution chamber in the usual manner and when he got immediately opposite the chair he started kicking but his arms had been held tight by additional officers that I had. The whole incident was greatly exaggerated in the newspapers because, of course, it was something out of the ordinary. However, there was no prolonged struggle to get him into the chair, and I would say that the incident didn't last over fifteen to twenty seconds before he was strapped in the usual manner. . . .

Very truly yours,
/S/
WARDEN

Ruth Snyder's electrocution, captured by hidden camera, January 12, 1928

LEGAL   ELECTROCUTION

JULIUS ROSENBERG, SS P:#110-649

TIME IN   TIME OUT   AMPS

8 04   8 06 3/4   8

ETHEL ROSENBERG, SSP:#110-510

TIME IN   TIME OUT   AMPS

8 11 1/2   8 14   6 1/2

Executioner's report card

Interior of death chamber.

Form M-52.—P.S. 99

STATE OF NEW YORK | DEPARTMENT OF CORRECTION

SING SING PRISON

NOTICE OF DEATH

No. 115-664   Name ROMULO, Rosario

Died 17 February, 1955   at   A. M.11:05 P. M.

Cause of Death LEGAL ELECTROCUTION

Physician H.W. Kipp, M.D. Jr. Physician

Typical death notice from Sing Sing

From Autopsy Report by M. S. Misielewicz, May 19, 1960:

The body is that of a well developed, muscular, colored male about 33 years of age. The body lies on the table in the usual position after execution. The head is back, the mouth is open, the eyes are staring and the right leg is drawn up about half-flexion. There are the usual seared marks revealing 2nd and 3rd degree burns on the dorsal part of the neck, and 2nd and 3rd degree burns on the dorsal part of the right knee. The right eye is missing. There is an operative scar in the lower right quadrant of the abdomen. Also, there is an operative scar of an old skin graft, donor area, measuring about 3 x 7 inches on the upper right thigh.

Western Union telegram, collect, May 20, 1960,
to Warden Denno from Buffalo:

SORRY TO ADVISE FAMILY IS FINANCIALLY UNABLE TO HANDLE BURIAL. THANK YOU. SIGNED MRS FLORENCE FLAKES.

Remains

From Autopsy Report, March 1, 1951, 11:15 P.M.
(following electrocution at 11:02 P.M.):

BRAIN: The brain weighed 1270 grams and is normal on sectioning. The brain and brain stem failed to show any pathology. On examination, the base and ball of the skull was stripped down and failed to show any significant remnant of a fracture. The dura is of normal color and thickness over the convexity. The cerebellum seen from the posterior surfaces is opaque and greyish in color. It has a boiled appearance. The whole brain is uncomfortably warm to the touch.

Typical telegram from the warden to the family of the deceased, reporting death

S.S.—Form 1-55

14-59-05

STATE OF NEW YORK—DEPARTMENT OF CORRECTION

SING SING PRISON

DCI No. 664-766 X

Name	Eddie Lee Mays	No. 130622 County	New York
Aliases	Eddie Lee May		
Term	EXECUTION	Date Sentenced 11-8-62	Date Received 11-8-62
Crime	Verd Murder 1st	Judge Irwin D. Davidson	Court Supreme

Criminal Act   Shot & killed Maria Marini .38 calibre pistol during stickup Friendly Bar and Grill night-and stole less than $100

Transfer

Discharge

Date of Crime 3-23-61   Age 33

Jail Time 223 days   Date of Birth 3-15-29   V

Height 5 ft. 7½ in.   pp't Age

Weight 131 lbs.   olor f eyes maroon

Build med slim   olor f Hair black

Nativity Walstonburg, NC   omplexion brown

Occupation Laborer   ar med

Amer Negro   ight Handed X

    eft Handed

    mbidextrous

Scars & Marks   light colored pigment in skin around both eyes arms and fingers

Associates   Bryant Brooks; Jose Fernandez; Joseph Sanchez; Keats Johnson

CRIMINAL HISTORY

Description taken by   Huguenin   Photograph taken by Huguenin   at SSP   Date 11-8-62

Eddie Lee Mays was the last person, the 695th, electrocuted by New York State.

Personal Property Left Behind by Inmate Ethel Rosenberg, #110–510:

1 Jar "Mum"
9 Commissary receipts
4 Note books (small)
2 Note books (very small)
1 Plastic soap box
1 Small can talcum powder
2 Powder puffs
1 Plastic bag (small)
1 Box face powder
1 Lip stick
3 Small combs
3 Barettes
1 Emory board

1. Six hard covered books
2. One soft covered book "They Shall Not Die"
3. Two soft covered books of songs
4. Webster's dictionary—hard cover
5. Two soft covered books, one French and one English
6. One soft covered book, "Give Us Your Hand" Segal
7. Carton marked with label saying: "Legal papers and clippings"
8. Hard backed photo class of '38 P.S. 70
9. Shoe box of letters (from children, relatives), also telegrams, letters from Death House, Julius & Ethel Rosenberg
10. Carton with label saying: "Cards, receipts, old letters"
11. Manila Envelopes containing copies of "National Guardian" and "Jewish Life" (3)
12. Three candy boxes of newspaper clippings
13. Ten loose leaf page note books in a carton
14. Two hard covered note books
15. Carton containing: 2 nylon stockings, 1 lyle stockings, 1 tandress, 2 bras, 2 woolie pants, 6 sox
16. One small white box of clothing
17. Small box of hankies
18. One box tan sandals

/s/
Thomas M. Farley, Chief Deputy
For WILLIAM A. CARROLL, US MARSHAL, SDNY

Personal Property Left Behind by Inmate Julius Rosenberg, #110–649:

1. July 4th, 1951 copy of Declaration of Independence
2. Cardboard with 6 of children's pictures
3. 8 Photos of children in small folder
4. Two pictures of Ethel cut from newspapers
5. 1953 Calendar
6. 1 box containing commissary receipts
7. 1 box of letters
8. Bags containing other letters and greeting cards received
9. Records and various legal papers on appeal, etc.
10. Complete file of National Guardian
11. Material published from Committee to Secure Justice
12. Jewish Life Magazines
13. Boxes of newspaper clippings on his case
14. His book of letters both in English and French
15. One copy of French newspaper with his story in serial form
16. A complete listing of each and every visit with Ethel, Family and Lawyer
17. A complete accounting of monies received and spent
18. 7 personal books hardcover
19. Various papers and memoranda

/S/
Thomas M. Farley, Chief Deputy
For WILLIAM A. CARROLL, US MARSHAL, SDNY

A. Provenzano
Licensed Undertaker
43 Second Ave. 240 Elizabeth Street
New York City
Grammercy 3-2220-1

July 3, 1944

Dear Mr. McCue:

Please send us two transcripts of death on Alex Bellomo, who died at Sing-Sing on June 29, 1944. If there is any charge let us know and we will forward check.

Thanking you
Mr. A. Provenzano

NAME:	Alex Bellomo
NUMBER:	102–655
AGE:	25
OCCUPATION:	Laborer
PHYSICAL:	5'6-¼", 126 lbs.
CRIME:	Shot Francis Servido in poolroom
ACCOMPLICES:	DeLitro, DiMaria
JUDGE:	Donnellan, New York General Sessions
SENTENCED:	10–25–43
RECEIVED:	11–8–43
EXECUTED:	6–29–44

Settling Up

SING SING PRISON
Ossining, N.Y.

June 9, 1961

To Whom It May Concern:

This is to certify that WOODROW MILLER received the last rites and sacraments of the Catholic Church and is, therefore, entitled to burial in consecrated ground.

Sincerely yours,
 (Rev.) George F. McKinney
Catholic Chaplain

Wednesday
August 13, 1958

Dear Warden Denno

I want to thank you, so very sincerely, for being so kind and thoughtful to me, in my hour of need. I shant ever forget how very good you've been.

When I started to write this there was so much I wanted to say & now I can't think of how to say anything. Warden, there was a paper I had to sign for you, or a "statement" I had to make? I did think you had said something like that to me, my brother-in-law had said, "it was all taken care of." I really don't remember.

My husband Angelo J. LaMarca had a "beautiful" mass said for us by Father McKinney & also the funeral services. It was all so *peaceful* and *quiet*, and again, I have you to thank for all that being possible.

Please, let me know if there was something I had to do for you, won't you? May God be with you—Always.

Most sincerely,
DONNA LAMARCA

NAME:	Angelo LaMarca
NUMBER:	120–110
AGE:	31
OCCUPATION:	Truck driver
MARITAL:	Married, 2 children
RELIGION:	Catholic
CRIME:	Kidnapped and murdered 1-month-old baby
CLAIMS:	I'm unable to answer that question
JUDGE:	Pittoni, Nassau County Court
SENTENCED:	12–14–56
RECEIVED:	12–14–56
EXECUTED:	8–7–58

August 16, 1954

Mr. Thomas J. Lunney
U.S. Marshal
Southern District of New York
U.S. Court House
Foley Square
New York 7, N.Y.

Dear Mr. Lunney:

I am attaching herewith vouchers executed by Mr. Dow B. Hower who officiated as legal executioner in the case of Gerhard A. Puff, #113970. One of these vouchers is in the amount of $150.00, which is the usual fee paid the executioner. The other is in the amount of $12.80 which covers mileage of 160 miles at the rate of eight cents per mile. You will note that the voucher covering the mileage does not give the starting point or the return point from Ossining. This is done in order to protect the locality in which the executioner resides as we do not desire his name nor his place of residence to become public knowledge through the press.

However, you can use my letter as certification to the effect that the mileage claimed by the executioner is the mileage which the State of New York pays him and is correct in all respects. Therefore, in order to protect the official residence of the executioner that is the reason why the starting point was not included in this bill.

If there are any questions in connection with this, I would ask that they be taken up with me instead of direct with Mr. Hover.

I might state that this same arrangement is in effect with the State of New York in that his address on all vouchers is given as 354 Hunter Street, Ossining, New York, which is the official street address of Sing Sing Prison.

Very truly yours,
/s/
WARDEN

WLD:cm
att.

May 11, 1953

Dear Madam:

In connection with your visit to my office on Thursday, May 7, 1953, in connection with the article entitled, "The Man Who Begged to Die" written by one Russel Travers in the July issue of the magazine Vital Detective Cases, pertaining to your brother, the late Edward Kelly, #109–821, who was confined in this institution until his legal execution on October 30, 1952 after conviction of the crime of Murder 1st degree.

I wish to advise you that the events describing his purported actions on the day of his execution as described in this article did not occur as narrated in this article, and it is apparent to me that the author of this article apparently has a vivid imagination or was misinformed.

Very truly yours,
/s/
WARDEN

Sing Sing Prison's graveyards along the river.

Prisoners Legally Executed
at Sing Sing Prison

Harris Alonzo Smiler, W, 32, NY, 7/7/1891

James Slocum, W, 22, NY, 7/7/91

Joseph Wood, B, 21, NY, 7/7/91

Shibaya Jugiro, A, 35, NY, 7/7/91

Martin D. Loppy, W, 51, NY, 12/7/91

Charles McElvaine, W, 20, Kings, 2/8/92

Jeremiah Cotto, W, 40, Kings, 3/28/92

Frederick McGuire, W, 24, Orange, 12/19/92

James L. Hamilton, B, 40, Queens, 4/3/93

Carlyle W. Harris, W, 23, NY, 5/8/93

John Lewis Osmond, W, 30, NY, 6/12/93

John Delfino, W, 26, Kings, 12/4/93

Matthew Johnson, B, 33, NY, 2/16/94

David Hampton, B, 27, NY, 1/28/95

Robert W. Buchanan, W, 31, NY, 7/1/95

Richard Leach, W, 31, NY, 8/5/95

Carl Feigenbaum, W, 54, NY, 4/14/96

Louis P. Hermann, W, 25, NY, 4/23/96

Charles Pustalka, W, 35, NY, 4/23/96

Arthur Mayhew, B, 26, Queens, 3/12/97

Howard A. Scott, B, 30, NY, 6/14/97

John Henry Barker, B, 42, Westchester, 7/6/97

Hadley A. Sutherland, B, 20, Kings, 1/10/98

Martin Thorn, W, 33, Queens, 8/1/98

Beilor Decker, B, 30, Richmond, 1/9/99

Martha Savacool Place, W, 44, Kings, 3/20/99

A = Asian, B = black, F = Filipino, W = white, NA = Native American

Adrian Braun, W, 38, Westchester, 5/29/99

Lewis Pullerson, B, 30, NY, 7/31/99

Michael McDonald, W, 24, NY, 7/31/99

Antonio Ferraro, W, 37, Kings, 2/26/1900

Constantine Steiger, aka Fritz Meyer, W, 46, NY, 5/21/00

Joseph Mullen, W, 30, NY, 7/23/00

William Neufeld, W, 27, NY, 1/14/01

Lorenzo Priori, W, 27, NY, 2/6/01

Benjamin Pugh, B, 21, Kings, 8/5/01

Joseph Zachello, W, 28, Richmond, 8/29/01

Aaron Halle, W, 24, NY, 8/4/02

Anthony Triola, W, 32, NY, 5/25/03

Arthur Flanagan, W, 27, NY, 6/8/03

Toni Turekofski, W, 32, Kings, 8/3/03

Patrick Conklin, W, 31, NY, 9/8/03

Carmine Gaimari, W, 31, NY, 11/23/03

William H. Ennis, W, 33, Kings, 12/14/03

Thomas Tobin, W, 38, NY, 3/14/04

Albert Koepping, W, 22, Orange, 6/13/04

Oscar Borgstrom, W, 55, Westchester, 6/13/04

Frank Henry Burness, W, 45, Kings, 6/27/04

William Spencer, W, 38, NY, 1/9/05

Frank Rimieri, W, 23, Kings, 2/20/05

Adolph Koenig, W, 23, NY, 2/20/05

Martin Ebelt, W, 24, Westchester, 4/10/05

Charles Jackson, B, 31, NY, 7/17/05

James Breen, W, 24, NY, 7/17/05

George Granger, W, 20, Dutchess, 2/25/07

Frank Furlong, W, 21, NY, 3/4/07

John J. Johnson, W, 37, Westchester, 6/24/07

William Nelson, B, 43, NY, 7/29/07

John Wenzel, W, 33, Kings, 11/18/07

A = Asian, B = black, F = Filipino, W = white, NA = Native American

Antonio Strollo, W, 24, NY, 3/9/08

Charles H. Rogers, W, 38, Orange, 7/20/08

Antonio Landiero, W, 27, NY, 7/20/08

Salvatore Governale, W, 25, NY, 2/1/09

William Jones, B, 27, Nassau, 3/8/09

Bernard Carlin, W, 22, Kings, 4/12/09

Bedros Hampartjoomian, W, 24, NY, 12/6/09

William Morse, B, 25, Kings, 1/3/10

John Barbuto, W, 24, Orange, 1/3/10

Carlo Giro, W, 35, Kings, 2/23/10

Charles Bowser, B, 38, NY, 2/28/10

Frederick Schleimann, aka John Smyth, W, 32, Kings, 3/14/10

Gilbert Coleman, B, 25, NY, 5/9/10

Carl Loos, W, 57, NY, 7/25/10

Giuseppe Gambaro, W, 43, NY, 7/25/10

Samuel Austin, B, 30, Westchester, 1/3/11

Frederick Gebhardt, aka Otto Mueller, W, 39, Suffolk, 6/12/11

Thomas Barnes, W, 38, Kings, 6/12/11

Giuseppe Samarco, W, 27, Westchester, 7/17/11

Robert Francis Wood, W, 27, NY, 7/17/11

Frank Schermerhorn, W, 23, Dutchess, 11/20/11

Pietro Falleta, W, 33, Westchester, 11/20/11

Bert L. Brown, B, 22, Westchester, 11/20/11

Philip Mangano, W, 53, NY, 1/8/12

Albert Wolter, W, 20, NY, 1/29/12

Charles Swenton, B, 29, NY, 2/5/12

Salvatore Condido, W, 27, Rockland, 5/6/12

Giuseppe Cerelli, W, 23, Westchester, 7/8/12

George Williams, B, 31, Westchester, 7/8/12

Santo Zanza, W, 25, Westchester, 7/8/12

John W. Collins, B, 23, NY, 8/12/12

Filepo DeMarco, W, 25, Westchester, 8/12/12

A = Asian, B = black, F = Filipino, W = white, NA = Native American

Vincenzo Cona, W, 22, Westchester, 8/12/12

Angelo Giusto, W, 22, Westchester, 8/12/12

Lorenzo L. Cali, W, 26, Westchester, 8/12/12

Salvatore DeMarco, W, 28, Westchester, 8/12/12

Joseph Ferrone, W, 30, NY, 8/12/12

Matteo Dellomo, W, 33, Kings, 12/16/12

Joseph Garfalo, W, 38, Suffolk, 2/10/13

George Bishop, B, 23, Kings, 2/10/13

Donato Cardillo, W, 22, Kings, 2/10/13

William Lingley, aka William Miller, W, 30, NY, 5/5/13

John Mulraney, W, 31, NY, 5/19/13

Gregorio Patini, W, 21, Westchester, 6/2/13

Andrea Manco, W, 28, Orange, 7/12/13

Antonio William Grace, W, 25, Orange, 8/4/13

Francis W. Mulchfeldt, W, 31, NY, 1/19/14

Harry Horowitz, W, 24, NY, 4/13/14

Frank Cirofici, W, 27, NY, 4/13/14

Jacob Seidenschmer, W, 21, NY, 4/13/14

Louis Rosenberg, W, 24, NY, 4/13/14

Pietro Repucci, W, 29, Westchester, 6/22/14

William Bressen, aka James McHenry, W, 27, Kings, 9/2/14

Joseph J. McKenna, W, 33, Kings, 9/2/14

Eng Hing, A, 20, NY, 2/5/15

Lee Dock, A, 30, NY, 2/5/15

Robert Kane, W, 28, Kings, 2/26/15

Vincenzo Campanelli, W, 36, NY, 2/26/15

Oscar Vogt, W, 37, NY, 2/26/15

Joseph Ferri, W, 37, Nassau, 2/26/15

Charles Becker, W, 43, NY, 7/30/15

Samuel Haynes, W, 43, NY, 7/30/15

Karol Draniewicz, W, 23, NY, 8/27/15

Thomas Tarpey, W, 42, Kings, 9/3/15

A = Asian, B = black, F = Filipino, W = white, NA = Native American

Pasquale Venditti, W, 47, Kings, 9/3/15

Antonio Salemne, W, 26, Monroe, 9/3/15

Louis M. Roach, W, 40, Montgomery, 9/3/15

William Perry, B, 27, NY, 9/3/15

Worthy Tolley, W, 49, Greene, 12/17/15

Ludwig Marquardt, W, 58, Ulster, 12/17/15

Antonio Ponton, W, 58, Schenectady, 12/17/15

Giuseppe Marendi, W, 28, Kings, 2/4/16

Hans Schmidt, W, 33, NY, 2/18/16

Walter Watson, W, 41, Kings, 3/3/16

Roy Champlain, W, 30, Allegheny, 6/2/16

Giovanni Supe, W, 31, Westchester, 6/2/16

Oreste Shillitoni, aka Harry Shields, W, 23, NY, 6/30/16

Allen Bradford, B, 29, NY, 8/4/16

Joseph Hanel, W, 36, Kings, 9/1/16

Jan Trybus, W, 33, Genesee, 9/1/16

Thomas O'Neil, aka Thomas Bambrick, W, 26, NY, 10/7/16

Charles Kumrow, W, 20, Erie, 12/19/16

Stanley J. Millstein, W, 19, Oneida, 12/19/16

Petrius C. von der Corput, W, 25, NY, 4/21/17

Antonio Impoluzzo, W, 20, NY, 5/17/17

Arthur Warren Waite, W, 29, NY, 5/24/17

Arthur Waltonen, W, 24, NY, 7/12/17

Joseph A. Mulholland, W, 29, NY, 8/30/17

Alex Schuster, aka Alexander Goldstein, W, 25, NY, 8/30/17

John Kushnieruk, W, 20, Essex, 5/23/18

Stephen Lischuk, W, 28, Essex, 6/13/18

Alvah Briggs, W, 25, St. Lawrence, 6/13/18

Hyman R. Stransky, W, 38, NY, 6/13/18

Johann Berg, W, 45, Kings, 7/18/18

Giuseppe Roberto, W, 23, Erie, 8/30/18

Carrl Van Poueke, W, 49, Bronx, 10/3/18

A = Asian, B = black, F = Filipino, W = white, NA = Native American

Jacob Cohen, W, 28, Kings, 12/19/18

Alton Cleveland, W, 36, Kings, 1/9/19

Giovanbatista Ferraro, W, 36, Cattaraugus, 3/21/19

Vincenzo Esposito, W, 31, Schenectady, 1/8/20

Gordon Fawcett Hamby, W, 27, Kings, 1/29/20

Richard Harrison, W, 26, NY, 5/13/20

Chester Cantine, W, 21, Dutchess, 5/13/20

Leo Jankowski, W, 26, Clinton, 5/28/20

Walter Levandowski, W, 25, Clinton, 5/28/20

James Montague Byrd, B, 26, Ulster, 7/22/20

Elmer Hyatt, W, 19, Monroe, 7/29/20

John P. Egan, W, 25, Bronx, 8/27/20

Frank Kelley, W, 40, Kings, 8/27/20

Walter Bojanowski, W, 26, Erie, 9/9/20

Howard Baker, W, 20, Wayne, 12/9/20

Joseph Usefof, W, 23, Bronx, 12/9/20

Joseph Milano, W, 22, Bronx, 12/9/20

Charles W. McLaughlin, W, 23, Bronx, 12/9/20

James P. Cassidy, W, 23, Bronx, 12/9/20

Enrique Garcia, W, 38, Cattaraugus, 1/27/21

Augustin L. Sanchez, W, 33, Cattaraugus, 1/27/21

Jesse Walker, W, 20, Kings, 2/10/21

Guy Nichols, W, 25, Kings, 3/13/21

James L. Odell, W, 24, Monroe, 4/29/21

Michael Casalino, W, 29, Queens, 5/5/21

John P. Bulgo, B, 27, Kings, 7/21/21

Angelo Giordano, W, 42, NY, 9/1/21

Harry B. Van Reed, W, 36, NY, 9/1/21

Edward J. McNally, W, 30, Richmond, 9/15/21

George Brazee, W, 59, Otsego, 12/15/21

William J. Marweg, W, 41, Erie, 1/12/22

Edward Persons, W, 41, Chautauqua, 1/12/22

A = Asian, B = black, F = Filipino, W = white, NA = Native American

Raymond F. Mulford, aka Roy Brown, W, 29, Erie, 1/12/22

Harry Givner, W, 27, Westchester, 2/2/22

Floyd E. Slover, aka Frank Barnes, W, 21, Erie, 2/2/22

George F. McCormick, W, 22, NY, 3/2/22

Lawrence Kubel, W, 37, Nassau, 3/23/22

Lawrence Torrence, W, 29, Erie, 4/20/22

Luigi Ebanista, W, 23, Rockland, 6/8/22

Albert Librero, W, 24, Rockland, 6/8/22

Julius Rothman, aka Julius Rosenwasser, W, 26, NY, 6/8/22

William Bell, B, 27, Queens, 6/15/22

Michael Rossi, W, 65, Westchester, 6/29/22

Saito Taizo, A, 23, NY, 7/20/22

Peter Nunziato, W, 28, Queens, 7/20/22

Herbert W. Smith, W, 33, Chenango, 8/31/22

Luther Boddy, B, 22, NY, 8/31/22

Henry Brown, B, 23, Bronx, 1/25/23

Joseph Zambelli, W, 25, Queens, 2/15/23

Alric J. Westling, W, 38, Bronx , 2/15/23

Anton Rabasovich, W, 34, Kings, 3/1/23

William J. Evans, W, 24, Richmond, 4/19/23

Michael Fradiano, W, 50, Bronx, 4/26/23

Joseph Alfano, W, 24, Queens, 4/26/23

Thomas Kindlon, W, 21, Albany, 6/7/23

Thomas Lester, W, 23, Albany, 6/7/23

Key Pendleton Smith, NA, 37, Kings, 6/22/23

Robert J. Blackstone, B, 27, Bronx, 7/12/23

Raeffaele Amendola, W, 34, Oneida, 8/30/23

Emilio Semione, W, 38, Erie, 12/6/23

Abraham Becker, W, 35, Bronx, 1/13/24

George William Hacker, Jr., W, 34, Broome, 1/13/24

Harry Santanello, W, 29, Broome, 1/13/24

Antonio Viadante, W, 41, Onondaga, 4/10/24

A = Asian, B = black, F = Filipino, W = white, NA = Native American

Reuben Norkin, W, 32, Bronx, 4/17/24

Albito Mastrota, W, 32, Queens, 6/12/24

Eulogia Lozado, F, 26, NY, 7/24/24

John Emieleta, W, 23, Suffolk, 1/8/25

John Rys, W, 19, Suffolk, 1/8/25

Edward Smith, W, 37, Erie, 1/15/25

Ambrose Geary, W, 38, Erie, 1/15/25

Harry Malcolm, W, 34, Erie, 1/15/25

Nick Ferranti, W, 44, Broome, 1/22/25

Florencio Lerma, W, 26, Erie, 1/22/25

John Thomas Leonard, W, 23, Bronx, 1/22/25

Patrick Murphy, W, 30, Erie, 3/12/25

Frank H. Minnick, W, 34, Erie, 3/12/25

Joseph Diamond, W, 22, Kings, 4/30/25

Morris Diamond, W, 28, Kings, 4/30/25

John Farina, W, 23, Kings, 4/30/25

John Durkin, W, 25, Bronx, 8/27/25

Julius Miller, B, 44, NY, 9/17/25

Luigi Rapito, W, 34, Cayuga, 1/29/26

Emil Klatt, W, 35, Westchester, 1/29/26

Matthew Wasser, W, 27, Niagara, 2/4/26

Ernest T. Mimms, B, 29, Bronx, 2/4/26

Frank A. Daley, W, 21, Westchester, 6/24/26

Sam Wing, A, 19, Kings, 7/15/26

William W. Hoyer, B, 26, NY, 8/19/26

David DeMaio, W, 34, Westchester, 8/19/26

John Garguila, W, 19, NY, 8/26/26

Cosimo Brescia, W, 19, Kings, 8/26/26

John J. Brennan, W, 28, Kings, 12/2/26

Kasimir Barszyouk, W, 21, Kings, 12/9/26

William Barszyouk, W, 28, Kings, 12/9/26

John Maxwell, W, 21, Kings, 12/9/26

A = Asian, B = black, F = Filipino, W = white, NA = Native American

George Williams, B, 27, NY, 1/6/27

Edgar Humes, B, 23, NY, 1/6/27

Charles Goldson, B, 23, NY, 1/6/27

Benjamin Bradley, B, 28, NY, 1/13/27

Mike Kosmowski, W, 36, Erie, 1/20/27

Paul E. Hilton, W, 27, Queens, 2/17/27

Anthony Paretti, W, 35, Kings, 2/17/27

Giuseppe Friia, W, 33, Monroe, 3/17/27

Giuseppe Provenzano, W, 24, Monroe, 3/17/27

William Wagner, W, 24, Kings, 7/14/27

Robert O'Neil, aka Peter Heslin, W, 28, NY, 7/21/27

Charles Albrecht, W, 33, NY, 9/29/27

Peter A. Seiler, W, 22, NY, 12/16/27

George A. Ricci, W, 33, Kings, 12/16/27

Louis Mason, B, 24, Erie, 1/5/28

Charles J. Doran, W, 25, Albany, 1/5/28

Ruth Brown Snyder, W, 33, Queens, 1/12/28

H. Judd Gray, W, 36, Queens, 1/12/28

Philip Ecker, W, 21, NY, 3/1/28

Frank Baldwin, B, 21, Seneca, 4/6/28

William Leroy Wagner, W, 24, Erie, 6/21/28

Joseph Lefkowitz, W, 30, Kings, 7/19/28

Ludwig Halverson Lee, W, 39, Kings, 8/2/28

Alexander Kalinowski, W, 50, Cayuga, 8/9/28

Daniel J. Graham, W, 26, NY, 8/9/28

George Appel, W, 41, Queens, 8/9/28

Martin Luther Miller, B, 32, Kings, 8/30/28

Thomas Moran, W, 20, Kings, 12/14/28

Israel Fischer, W, 19, Kings, 1/24/29

Isidore Helfant, W, 21, Kings, 1/24/29

Harry Dreitzer, W, 23, Kings, 1/24/29

John Fabri, W, 31, Onondaga, 8/29/29

A = Asian, B = black, F = Filipino, W = white, NA = Native American

Frank Kowalski, W, 25, Erie, 1/2/30

Arthur Brown, W, 34, Erie, 1/2/30

John E. Schlager, W, 32, Erie, 1/9/30

Frank Plaia, W, 20, Nassau, 1/30/30

Michael Sclafonia, W, 20, Nassau, 1/30/30

Stephen Ziolkowski, W, 20, Erie, 5/29/30

Stephen Grzechowiak, W, 29, Erie, 7/17/30

Max Rybarczyk, W, 31, Erie, 7/17/30

Alex Bogdanoff, W, 35, Erie, 7/17/30

William Force, W, 28, Cayuga, 8/28/30

Claude Udwin, W, 29, Cayuga, 8/28/30

Jesse Thomas, W, 20, Cayuga, 8/28/30

James Bolger, W, 19, Nassau, 12/12/30

James Butler, W, 20, Nassau, 12/12/30

Italo Ferdinandi, W, 22, Nassau, 12/12/30

Anthony Velluchio, W, 40, Montgomery, 2/26/31

Anthony Luciano, W, 36, Montgomery, 2/26/31

Haywood Turner, B, 29, Bronx, 6/25/31

Fred Innes, B, 38, Bronx, 6/25/31

Fred Carmosino, W, 19, Bronx, 7/2/31

Ferdinand Mangiamele, W, 34, Bronx, 7/2/31

Nicholas Leonelli, W, 23, Bronx, 7/2/31

Andrew P. Metelski, W, 21, Erie, 7/23/31

Herbert Johnson, B, 19, Schoharie, 7/23/31

Harry Lipschitz, W, 25, Westchester, 8/27/31

Maurice Seaton, B, 42, NY, 9/4/31

Rudolph Duringer, W, 26, Bronx, 12/10/31

Alphonse Carrato, W, 41, Westchester, 1/7/32

Giuseppe Caricari, W, 27, Westchester, 1/7/32

Joseph Senna, W, 32, Bronx, 1/14/32

Francis Crowley, W, 19, Nassau, 1/21/32

Gavino Delmiar, aka George Damico, F, 32, Kings, 1/28/32

A = Asian, B = black, F = Filipino, W = white, NA = Native American

Peter Sardini, W, 28, Kings, 3/31/32

Dominic Scifo, W, 24, Queens, 3/31/32

Michael Rodrick, W, 20, Queens, 3/31/32

Walter Borowsky, W, 24, Queens, 3/31/32

John Dawson, B, 35, NY, 6/9/32

Frank Giordano, W, 32, Bronx, 7/2/32

Dominic Odierno, W, 20, Bronx, 7/2/32

Alfred Corbellini, W, 21, NY, 7/15/32

Alfred Cozzi, W, 20, NY, 7/15/32

Luigi Raffa, W, 36, Bronx, 7/22/32

Louis Katoff, W, 27, Bronx, 7/22/32

Frank Mayo, W, 29, Bronx, 7/22/32

Leon Blecharsky, aka George Harris, W, 35, NY, 9/2/32

Charles Markowitz, W, 21, NY, 12/10/32

Joseph Brown, W, 20, NY, 12/10/32

Peter Harris, W, 21, Cattaraugus, 1/12/33

Thomas Carpenter, B, 19, Bronx, 1/12/33

Charles Bates, B, 19, Bronx, 1/12/33

Alexander Nunes, W, 44, Westchester, 1/19/33

William Turner, W, 22, NY, 2/2/33

Bruno Korchinsky, aka Bruno Polowicz, W, 36, Niagara, 4/20/33

Alex Kasprzcak, W, 39, Niagara, 4/20/33

Angelo Lopez, W, 26, NY, 5/25/33

William H. Jackson, B, 40, Niagara, 6/1/33

Nathaniel Covington, B, 28, NY, 7/13/33

Stephen R. Witherell, W, 30, St. Lawrence, 8/17/33

John Jordan, W, 33, Queens, 8/17/33

George Swan, W, 21, Queens, 8/17/33

Alex Carrion, W, 27, Bronx, 8/24/33

Frank Negron, W, 25, Bronx, 8/24/33

Harry Edmunds, B, 50, Bronx, 9/1/33

John Tinsley, B, 25, Bronx, 9/1/33

A = Asian, B = black, F = Filipino, W = white, NA = Native American

John McKinney, B, 42, Suffolk, 9/1/33

Winston C. Owens, B, 34, NY, 1/11/34

Joseph Willis, B, 24, NY, 1/11/34

Herman Cunningham, B, 23, NY, 1/11/34

Lloyd Price, B, 22, Kings, 3/1/44

Frank Pasqua, W, 24, Bronx, 6/7/34

Anthony Marino, W, 27, Bronx, 6/7/34

Daniel Kriesberg, W, 29, Bronx, 6/7/34

William Vogel, W, 26, NY, 6/14/34

Ross Caccamise, W, 24, Monroe, 6/14/34

Joseph Murphy, W, 27, Bronx, 7/5/34

Frank Canora, W, 51, Rockland, 7/12/34

Anna Antonio, W, 27, Albany, 8/9/34

Sam Faracci, W, 42, Albany, 8/9/34

Vincent Saeta, W, 33, Albany, 8/9/34

Alphonse Brengard, W, 29, Nassau, 9/6/34

Harold Seaman, W, 21, Kings, 1/10/35

Vincent Walsh, W, 21, NY, 1/10/35

Frank Mitchell, W, 26, NY, 1/17/35

Giuseppe Leonti, W, 43, NY, 1/24/35

William Paskowitz, W, 26, Bronx, 2/7/35

Peter Crotty, W, 26, Bronx, 2/7/35

Alfred Giallarenzi, W, 30, Onondaga, 2/7/35

Vincent DeLeo, W, 29, Clinton, 2/21/35

Bruno Salek, W, 20, Erie, 4/25/35

Stanley Pluzdrak, W, 17, Erie, 4/25/35

Eva Coo, W, 41, Otsego, 6/27/35

Leonard Scarnici, W, 27, Schoharie, 6/27/35

Patrick Downey, W, 31, Suffolk, 7/11/35

Alfred C. Lindsay, W, 29, Cattaraugus, 8/29/35

Percy Morris, B, 29, Bronx, 12/5/35

Jefferson Brown, B, 22, Bronx, 12/5/35

A = Asian, B = black, F = Filipino, W = white, NA = Native American

Raymond Newman, W, 22, NY, 1/9/36

Amerigo Angelini, W, 23, NY, 1/9/36

Thomas Rooney, aka Tom Gilbride, W, 23, NY, 1/9/36

Raymond Orlikowski, aka Ray Orley, W, 22, NY, 1/9/36

John Smith, B, 41, Bronx, 1/16/36

Albert H. Fish, W, 66, Westchester, 1/16/36

Francis A. Flynn, W, 39, Queens, 2/27/36

Peter Mohlsick, W, 20, Westchester, 4/16/36

Howard Eichler, W, 21, Westchester, 4/16/36

Nicholas Buckvich, W, 42, Monroe, 4/23/36

Charles Kropowitz, W, 22, Kings, 5/28/36

George Rosenberg, W, 22, Kings, 5/28/36

Frank Russo, W, 24, Kings, 5/28/36

Vincent DeMartino, W, 27, Kings, 5/28/36

Damiano Consentino, W, 39, Kings, 6/4/36

John Collins, W, 26, Queens, 7/9/36

Frances Avery Creighton, W, 36, Nassau, 7/16/36

Everett C. Appelgate, W, 36, Nassau, 7/16/36

Raymond Flores, W, 26, NY, 7/23/36

Theodore McFarland, W, 38, Kings, 8/20/36

Charles Rogas, W, 35, Kings, 8/27/36

Theodore DiDionne, W, 31, Kings, 1/7/37

Joseph Bolognia, W, 24, Kings, 1/14/37

Louis Lazar, W, 29, Kings, 1/14/37

Charles Hamm, B, 19, Kings, 1/21/37

Frederick Fowler, B, 18, Kings, 1/21/37

Chester White, B, 33, Nassau, 1/21/37

John Fiorenza, W, 25, NY, 1/21/37

Alfred D. Volkmann, W, 20, Greene, 2/11/37

Chew Wing, A, 32, NY, 6/10/37

Harry Eisenberg, W, 43, Kings, 7/1/37

Watson Edwards, W, 25, Kings, 7/1/37

A = Asian, B = black, F = Filipino, W = white, NA = Native American

Anthony Garlaus, W, 33, Kings, 7/1/37

Major Green, B, 33, Queens, 8/19/37

Louis Apicello, W, 40, Kings, 8/26/37

Salvatore Ossido, W, 27, Kings, 1/6/38

Charles James Brown, B, Ulster, 2/24/38

Terrence Roberts, W, 30, NY, 5/26/38

Lawrence Marks, W, 50, Kings, 6/2/38

George Lewis, W, 25, Kings, 8/11/38

Felix J. Cummings, W, 27, Kings, 8/11/38

John Rylowicz, aka Johnny Reo, W, 39, Nassau, 8/18/38

David Lucas, B, 29, Niagara, 1/5/39

Salvatore Gati, W, 29, NY, 1/5/39

Charles Sberna, W, 29, NY, 1/5/39

Vincente Forte, W, 19, Kings, 1/12/39

Arthur Friedman, W, 21, NY, 1/26/39

Dominick Guariglia, W, 18, NY, 1/26/39

Joseph H. O'Laughlin, W, 23, NY, 1/26/39

Thomas K. Gilmore, W, 42, Orange, 2/9/39

Michael Hermanowski, W, 24, Suffolk, 2/16/39

Thomas Bohan, W, 34, NY, 2/16/39

Michael Alex, W, 28, NY, 2/23/39

Arthur Perry, B, 24, Queens, 8/24/39

Theodore Maselkiewicz, W, 53, Erie, 12/21/39

Everett McDonald, B, 40, NY, 12/21/39

Anton Myslivec, W, Suffolk, 12/21/39

Anselmo Abreu, W, 41, Bronx, 1/4/40

Joseph S. Sacoda, W, 28, NY, 1/11/40

Demetrius Gula, W, 27, NY, 1/11/40

Sidney Markmam, W, 21, Kings, 1/18/40

Frank Jenner, W, 21, Onondaga, 2/15/40

John Kulka, W, 24, NY, 2/15/40

Bertal Thingstead, W, 29, NY, 2/15/40

A = Asian, B = black, F = Filipino, W = white, NA = Native American

Gus Schweinberger, W, 30, Westchester, 4/25/40

Oliver R. Alridge, B, 47, Cattaraugus, 7/11/40

James Pryor, B, 23, NY, 7/11/40

Norman Wheelock, W, 27, Steuben, 8/1/40

Benjamin Ertrel, W, 25, NY, 9/12/40

Frank Blazek, W, 30, Bronx, 9/12/40

Major Greenfield, B, 33, Bronx, 1/9/41

Norman Williams, B, 32, NY, 2/6/41

Eugene Brown, B, 26, NY, 2/6/41

Archangelo D'Agosto, W, 27, Kings, 2/13/41

Walter Dowling, aka James Kearns, W, 21, Kings, 2/13/41

George Dolny, W, 22, Kings, 2/13/41

Joseph P. Carosella, W, 26, Nassau, 2/20/41

Hyman Balatniecov, W, 28, NY, 2/20/41

David Adler, W, 26, NY, 2/20/41

David Salemi, W, 33, Kings, 6/5/41

Martin Goldstein, W, 35, Kings, 6/12/41

Harry Strauss, W, 31, Kings, 6/12/41

Dewey Garrett, B, 21, NY, 7/10/41

Stanley Cole, W, 35, NY, 7/10/41

George Zeitz, W, 25, Kings, 9/18/41

Isaac Richardson, B, 28, NY, 1/8/42

Ralph G. Jones, B, 35, NY, 1/15/42

Henry Anerum, B, 31, NY, 1/15/42

Arthur Renna, W, 36, Bronx, 1/22/42

Thomas Conroy, W, 39, Bronx, 1/29/42

Frank Abbendando, W, 31, Kings, 2/19/42

Harry Maione, W, 32, Kings, 2/19/42

George Joseph Cvek, W, 24, Bronx, 2/26/42

Morris Mardevich, W, 24, NY, 3/5/42

Anthony Esposito, aka Angelo DiStefano, W, 36, NY, 3/12/42

William Esposito, aka Joseph DiStefano, W, 29, NY, 3/12/42

A = Asian, B = black, F = Filipino, W = white, NA = Native American

Joseph Riordan, W, 26, Westchester, 6/11/42

Charles McGale, W, 45, Westchester, 6/11/42

Carlo Barone, W, 27, Kings, 9/10/42

Edward Hicks, B, 21, Kings, 9/10/42

Lawrence Edwards, B, 18, NY, 9/27/42

Manuel Jacinto, W, 23, Orange, 9/27/42

James Clark, B, 21, NY, 9/27/42

Edmund Sileo, W, 27, Kings, 1/14/43

Joseph Sonsky, W, 32, NY, 1/14/43

Frank Castellano, W, 26, NY, 1/21/43

Angelo Mendez, W, 30, NY, 1/21/43

Eli E. Shonbrun, aka Ted Leopold, W, 33, NY, 2/29/43

John Cullen, W, 45, NY, 2/29/43

Harold J. Elling, W, 20, NY, 3/4/43

Benitez DeJesus, B, 18, NY, 7/8/43

Edward Haight, W, 17, Westchester, 7/8/43

Guillermo Diaz, aka William Diaz, B, 18, NY, 7/8/43

Alfred Haynes, B, 26, Kings, 7/15/43

Anibal Almodovar, 21, NY, 9/16/43

Joseph C. Mascari, W, 32, Madison, 1/6/44

Herbert Lewis, B, 35, Kings, 1/13/44

Louis Valle, W, 43, Nassau, 1/21/44

John Regan, W, 33, NY, 2/10/44

Joseph Palma, aka Joe Palmer, W, 27, Kings, 3/2/44

Vincent Soolami, W, 26, Kings, 3/2/44

Louis Capone, W, 48, Kings, 3/2/44

Emanuel Weiss, W, 38, Kings, 3/2/44

Louis "Lepke" Buchalter, W, 47, Kings, 3/2/44

John Ranford, B, 40, Nassau, 5/25/44

Louis Parisi, W, 24, NY, 6/3/44

Winston A. Sealy, B, 21, Kings, 6/22/44

Gordon Cooke, B, 19, Kings, 6/22/44

A = Asian, B = black, F = Filipino, W = white, NA = Native American

Frank DiMaria, W, 23, NY, 6/29/44

Alex Bellomo, W, 25, NY, 6/29/44

Peter DeLutro, W, 23, NY, 6/29/44

Lew York Hing, A, 18, NY, 8/31/44

Yun Tieh Li, 24, NY, 8/31/44

Helen Fowler, B, 37, Niagara, 11/16/44

George Franklin Knight, B, 26, Niagara, 11/16/44

Oliver Little, B, 22, NY, 1/17/46

George W. Donaldson, W, 48, Rensselaer, 3/7/46

Abraham Gold, W, 44, Kings, 4/25/44

Louis Dwight Brookins, W, 21, Monroe, 9/12/46

Henry Paul Suckow, W, 24, Queens, 3/6/47

Edward E. Koberski, W, 22, Queens, 3/6/47

Edward Kahkoska, W, 22, Queens, 3/6/47

Arthur Johnson, B, 21, Kings, 4/17/47

William Washington, B, 28, Kings, 4/17/47

Ward Beecher Caraway, B, 22, Nassau, 7/3/47

Salvatore DiCristofaro, W, 36, Erie, 7/10/47

Edward Jones, B, 23, Kings, 7/10/47

Arnold Sims, B, 23, Kings, 7/10/47

William James Thomas, B, 20, NY, 7/10/47

Webster Daniels, B, 37, NY, 8/21/47

Enix Bussey, B, 31, NY, 12/4/47

Jauvhan Jackson, B, 18, Kings, 1/8/48

Anthony R. Papa, W, 27, Nassau, 7/1/48

Raymond Haughton, aka Lester Haughton, B, 24, Bronx, 7/22/48

George C. Moore, B, 34, Bronx, 7/22/48

Milton Shaket, W, 34, NY, 9/16/48

John Reilly, W, 32, NY, 9/16/48

Harris Gray, B, 18, NY, 1/6/49

Louis Smiley, B, 19, NY, 1/13/49

Eugene Pannell, B, 27, NY, 1/20/49

A = Asian, B = black, F = Filipino, W = white, NA = Native American

Willie Grant, B, 24, NY, 1/20/49

George L. Monge, B, 23, NY, 1/20/49

Santo Bretagna, W, 27, NY, 3/3/49

William Rosenberg, W, 42, NY, 3/3/49

William Dupree, B, 32, NY, 6/30/49

Harold Dupree, B, 27, NY, 6/30/49

John M. Dunn, W, 36, NY, 7/7/49

Andrew Sheridan, W, 56, NY, 7/7/49

William M. Jackson, B, 23, NY, 9/1/49

Floyd Arrington, B, 22, NY, 9/1/49

Walter Davis, B, 21, Kings, 9/8/49

Frank Bruno, W, 31, Kings, 1/5/50

George Peter Reeh, W, 31, NY, 1/12/50

Julio Ramirez Perez, W, 36, NY, 5/25/50

Harley G. LaMarr, NA, 19, Erie, 1/11/51

William Winston Bunch, B, 21, Nassau, 2/15/51

Gilberto C. Walker, B, 26, NY, 3/1/51

John Joseph King, W, 21, Queens, 3/8/51

Richard J. J. Powers, W, 21, Queens, 3/8/51

Raymond M. Fernandez, W, 34, Bronx, 3/8/51

Martha Jule Beck, W, 29, Bronx, 3/8/51

John Saiu, W, 38, Bronx, 4/12/51

Bernard Stein, W, 35, NY, 3/6/52

Wallace Perry Ford, Jr., B, 31, Genesee, 10/30/52

Edward H. Kelly, W, 53, Ulster, 10/30/52

Joseph L. Paonessa, W, 42, Dutchess, 1/15/53

Stephen D. Lewis, W, 42, Dutchess, 1/22/53

Frank Wojcik, W, 56, Wyoming, 4/16/53

Julius Rosenberg, W, 37, Federal, 6/19/53

Ethel Rosenberg, W, 35, Federal, 6/19/53

Donald Hugh Snyder, W, 26, Putnam, 7/16/53

William H. Draper, W, 34, Monroe, 1/7/54

A = Asian, B = black, F = Filipino, W = white, NA = Native American

Maurice O'Dell, W, 28, Erie, 1/7/54

Walter Griffin, W, 26, Erie, 1/7/54

John Martin, B, 29, Kings, 3/11/54

Henry Louis Allen, B, 19, Kings, 3/11/54

Emil Hendrick Scott, B, 21, NY, 7/15/54

William Van der Wyde, W, 40, NY, 7/22/54

Gerhard A. Puff, W, 40, Federal, 8/12/54

John Dale Green, B, 24, Bronx, 8/26/54

Barry Jacobs, W, 22, Bronx, 8/26/54

Henry Matthews, W, 18, NY, 2/10/55

Romulo Rosario, W, 38, NY, 2/17/55

Nathan Wissner, W, 43, Westchester, 7/9/55

Harry A. Stein, W, 57, Westchester, 7/9/55

Calman Cooper, W, 47, Westchester, 7/9/55

Clarence M. Reed, W, 32, NY, 9/8/55

Edward J. Nichols, B, 28, NY, 9/8/55

William Byers, aka William David Snyder, W, 19, NY, 1/12/56

Norman Roye, B, 17, NY, 1/19/56

John Francis Roche, W, 28, NY, 1/26/56

Ernest Lee Edwards, W, 22, Kings, 6/28/56

Frank J. Newman, W, 51, Nassau, 8/23/56

Joseph Reade, W, 27, Chautauqua, 8/30/56

Leonardo Salemi, W, 44, NY, 2/28/57

MacDonald F. Browne, W, 31, Bronx, 3/14/57

Miguel Santiago, W, 29, NY, 8/15/57

David Taylor, B, 44, Bronx, 11/21/57

Elmer Francis Burke, W, 40, NY, 1/9/58

Nicholas Dan, Jr., B, 20, Niagara, 7/3/58

Angelo John LaMarca, W, 33, Nassau, 8/7/58

Virgil Richardson, B, 29, Queens, 11/20/58

Edward Eckwerth, W, 31, Westchester, 5/22/59

Jackson Turner, Jr., B, 23, Queens, 7/16/59

A = Asian, B = black, F = Filipino, W = white, NA = Native American

Ralph Dawkins, B, 22, Queens, 7/16/59
Leroy Keith, B, 52, Bronx, 7/23/59
Ivory Mason, B, 40, NY, 1/14/60
Pablo Vargas, W, 35, NY, 5/12/60
Walter T. Green, B, 33, Erie, 5/19/60
Henry Flakes, B, 33, Erie, 5/19/60
Willard Hodge Phillips, B, 44, Nassau, 6/23/60
Ronald Chapman, B, 20, NY, 12/1/60
Ralph Downs, B, 28, Bronx, 1/5/61
Woodrow Miller, B, 32, Kings, 6/8/61
Frederick Charles Wood, W, 51, Queens, 3/21/63
Eddie Lee Mays, B, 34, NY, 8/15/63

A = Asian, B = black, F = Filipino, W = white, NA = Native American

About the Author

Scott Christianson is the author of *With Liberty for Some: 500 Years of Imprisonment in America* (1998), winner of the 1999 Robert F. Kennedy Book Award Distinguished Honors. He lives near Albany, New York.